Mallard

STEAMING INTO IMMORTALITY

MALLARD

STEAMING INTO IMMORTALITY

ROBIN JONES

First published as Mallard 75, 2013, and Mallard — The Magnificent Six, 2014
by Mortons Media Group

This edition published in 2021 by Gresley Books,
an imprint of Mortons Books Ltd.
Media Centre
Morton Way
Horncastle LN9 6JR
www.mortonsbooks.co.uk

ISBN 978-1-911658-21-4

The right of Robin Jones to be identified as the author of this work has been
asserted in accordance with the Copyright, Designs and Patents Act 1988.

Typeset by Jayne Clements (jayne@hinoki.co.uk), Hinoki Design and Typesetting.
Printed and bound by Gutenberg Press, Malta.

10 9 8 7 6 5 4 3 2 1

*To my brother Stuart, who inspired me with all things
steam on steel wheels at an early age.*

Contents

Introduction

T HIS IS the story of not only one of the greatest British transport legends of all time, but also of the ground-breaking and indeed world-shrinking moves that were made to celebrate the 75th anniversary of its finest hour.

It was on July 3, 1938, that Sir Nigel Gresley's LNER A4 Pacific No. 4468 *Mallard* claimed what became an all-time world steam railway speed record.

The 35 magnificent art deco aerodynamically-streamlined A4 4-6-2s were the brainchild of chief mechanical engineer Sir Nigel Gresley, one of the greatest of all steam locomotive designers. However, it was ordinary people who elevated *Mallard* to its immortal stardom.

Daredevil Doncaster driver Joe Duddington, his fireman Thomas Bray and inspector Sam Jenkins took No. 4468 to an international headline-grabbing 126mph on the East Coast Main Line when passing the remarkably unspoilt Lincolnshire village of Little Bytham.

The exact spot of their achievement — coming 136 years after another Briton, Richard Trevithick, built the world's first steam locomotive — is now marked by a steel sign above the cutting where the top speed was recorded by the dynamometer car behind.

The footplate trio became celebrities overnight, but were back at work the following day carrying out their normal duties. They may not have been rewarded with the glamorous champagne-popping lifestyle of today's rich and famous, but their names nonetheless entered railway folklore along with that of Gresley, whose dream of taking an A4 to 130mph and maybe beyond was shattered by the start of the Second World War.

Gresley's cutting-edge A4s, however, continued to give sterling service until times moved on again and they were replaced by modern diesels in the form of the Class 55 Deltics and others.

Yet the A4s were never gone, nor forgotten, and examples have been seen in regular service in modern times, thanks to enthusiasts who saved them from the scrapyard, restored then to running order and returned them to the national network as soon as they were permitted to do so. To mark the half-centenary of the record in 1988, *Mallard* was returned to working order and hauled several main line specials.

When it came to celebrating 75 years since that magnificent display of derring-do on Stoke Bank however, officials of the engine's owner the National Railway Museum decided that there was no business case for another A4 to be restored. At the time there were three running on the national network and this was considered sufficient to satisfy the available railtour workload.

So what could be done to mark the anniversary? Steve Davies, then director of the NRM, had a flash of inspiration. Why not bring all six surviving A4s together for the first and possibly the only time in the post steam age? "Mission impossible" was the immediate response from many observers both inside the railway heritage sector and outside.

In the dying years of steam, when the A4s were being withdrawn from service and sent for scrap, one of them, No. 60008 *Dwight D. Eisenhower*, was acquired by the US National Railroad Museum at Green Bay in Wisconsin. None other than that famous axeman, Dr Richard Beeching, in his capacity as British Railways chairman, handed it over to the US ambassador to Britain on April 27, 1964, the day it left our shores seemingly forever.

Sister engine No. 60010 *Dominion of Canada* had similar luck, also saved from the cutter's torch by virtue of its name. It was acquired by the

Canadians' equivalent of Green Bay, the Exporail museum in Montreal.

It is indeed sad that such a fate did not befall other members of the class such as *Dominion of New Zealand* or *Commonwealth of Australia*.

Back in the Sixties, the British railway preservation movement, deemed to have begun on May 7, 1951, when the Talyllyn Railway ran its first services following a takeover by volunteers, was still very much in its early stages, and we were fortunate that three survived in the UK addition to *Mallard*, saved as part of the National Collection by virtue of its golden moment.

As the UK heritage sector matured, many approaches were made to both American museums to see if they were willing to sell their A4s back to Britain. Each offer was firmly rejected.

Some British enthusiasts made a pilgrimage to the museums to see one or both on static display – and visits to Green Bay and Exporail are heartily recommended. However, they remained lost to the majority of Brits who did not have the time or money to hop across the Atlantic for that purpose. Indeed, several generations have passed since they were shipped abroad.

Steve Davies, however, produced a new offer which struck a chord: Let the NRM borrow the pair for two years – and in return they will be cosmetically restored.

Dwight D. Eisenhower would get a new coat of Brunswick green livery, while *Dominion of Canada* would be retro-converted to its original LNER form, in garter blue livery with valances and with that Canadian National Railroad bell restored both in position on the front and to working order.

It was easier said than done. Not only was there the problem of shipping the pair across North America and by boat to Liverpool, but also the biggest stumbling block was that *Dwight D. Eisenhower* had been all but bricked up inside its museum shed.

What followed was a truly inspirational tale of transatlantic determination to complete the 'impossible' mission. In its own way, the story of the temporary repatriation of *Dwight D. Eisenhower* and *Dominion of Canada* is as incredible as that of *Mallard's* world steam speed record. The operation produced a stupendous level of co-operation between the NRM, Green Bay and Exporail, and was achieved at less than a third of the full commercial cost thanks to hugely generous sponsorship deals.

The end result was the first of three Great Gatherings; the line-up of all six survivors around the former York North shed turntable, now the Great Hall of the NRM at York, from July 3-17, 2013.

On the opening day, a Wednesday outside the peak holiday season when most people would be at work, around 7000 visitors turned up. York was literally heaving, as were internet servers. The museum's Facebook page received 130,000 views, and demand to access its nrm.org.uk website was so great that countless surfers were unable to call it up.

Saturday, July 6, saw 13,035 people visit the museum, a record for a single day. And the following day, despite a heatwave and Andy Murray's Wimbledon championship-winning final on TV, nearly 8000 people turned up. Overall, in the first five days, nearly 43,000 visited. Local newspaper *The Press*, York, enthused: "Never in York's long history has there been a family reunion quite like it.

"Forget the Rolling Stones at Glastonbury. The Great Gathering of the six surviving A4 locomotives at the National Railway Museum was the most spectacular assembly of ageing stars you could wish for."

Mallard 75's patron Prince Charles arranged a private visit on Monday, July 22, to see both the record breaker and the repatriated pair, after the three operational A4s had left the line-up five days earlier.

The event was scheduled to be followed by *Mallard's* first visit to Grantham in 50 years for a steam festival at the station on September 8-9, supported by *Heritage Railway* and *The Railway Magazine*, and an Autumn Great Gathering at York on October 26-November 8, when the line-up was again scheduled to be staged after the three operational A4s had completed another round of 21st century steam duties.

Finally, the Locomotion museum at Shildon, to which *Dwight D. Eisenhower* and *Dominion of Canada* were taken immediately after they arrived at Liverpool Docks in early October 2012, was the venue chosen for the Great Goodbye from February 15-23. That event proved to be an emotional farewell to the pair before their return to their North American homes, possibly forever.

Much has been written about *Mallard* and the A4s over the years. This, for the first time, is the complete story; from the world's first ever Pacific locomotives to the world steam speed records set by *Flying Scotsman* and then *Mallard* to one of the biggest highlights heritage era. It covers *Mallard's* latter-day British Railways career and its return to steam in preservation, as well as a detailed history of the other five survivors, and outlines the story of how the exiled pair came home to be restored to their true glory.

The A4s are living legends; three are still very much running, and one of them, *Bittern*, set a new official UK preservation era steam record of 92.5mph just five days before the Great Gathering began.

I am certain this will not be the final word. By the time Mallard 100 comes around, there are likely to be many more chapters to add.

Robin Jones

CHAPTER 1

The Pacific Highway

T HE STEAM railway locomotive was not only a British invention, but one which was honed to perfection above all others, with A4 *Mallard* claiming the world speed record of 126mph on Stoke Bank on July 3, 1938.

The world's first railway locomotive, designed by Cornish mining engineer Richard Trevithick, was built at Coalbrookdale 136 years earlier in 1802. Two years later, he gave the first public demonstration of a railway locomotive on the Penydarren Tramroad near Merthyr Tydfil.

Trevithick's big breakthrough, one which took the finer fruits of the Industrial Revolution to new heights, was the cylindrical boiler, which made all high-pressure steam applications possible, and not just railway locomotives.

The biggest leap forward in the development of the modern steam locomotive was the design of George and Robert Stephenson's *Rocket*, which won the Rainhill Trials in 1829. It was the first of the early engines to bring together several innovations, such as a single pair of driving wheels, multiple boiler fire tubes, a blastpipe, cylinders directly connected to driving wheels and closer to the horizontal and a separate firebox. Taken together, these features not only resulted in the most advanced locomotive of its time but also set in stone the way forward for other designers to follow. Indeed, *Rocket* was a blueprint for locomotive design that would be perpetuated right up to the end of steam.

There were, of course, countless other landmark developments in the evolution of the steam locomotive as engineers and railway companies competed with each other for greater pulling power, speed, efficiency and reliability, and it would take an encyclopaedia of encyclopaedias to list them all.

However, when detailing the history of the locomotive that set an all-time world speed record, the story has to begin with one particular milestone. That happened in 1901 and this time it did not involve a British innovation. That year the world's first 4-6-2, designed with a large firebox, was ordered by the New Zealand Railways Department from the Baldwin Locomotive Works of Philadelphia, Pennsylvania.

The department's chief mechanical engineer A L Beattie ordered 13 Q class locomotives, each with a firebox big enough to burn poor grade lignite coal from the eastern South Island mines. However, they were not the earliest 4-6-2s. In 1887 the Lehigh Valley Railroad in the US experimented with a 4-6-0 by adding a 'Strong's patent firebox' to it. This was a cylindrical device behind the cab which needed an extension of the frame and the addition of two trailing wheels to support it.

Two years later, the Chicago, Milwaukee and St Paul Railway rebuilt a conventional 4-6-0 with trailing wheels in order to reduce its axle load. Six Q class 4-6-2 tank locomotives were introduced on the Western Australian Government Railways in 1896. However, none of these is considered to be a true Pacific locomotive in the modern sense of the word.

But why 'Pacific'? The 4-6-2 was an evolution of Baldwin's 4-4-2 Atlantic type, but it is also said that a New Zealand designer first proposed the Pacific design. Another theory is that the name was taken from the Missouri Pacific Railroad which used many 4-6-2s in the Twenties. It very quickly became obvious that Baldwin and the New Zealand Railways Department were on to a winner with Pacifics.

They were superbly equipped for high-speed running. The four-wheel leading truck provided increased stability at speed, the six driving wheels permitted a larger boiler and greater tractive effort than an Atlantic, while the two-wheel trailing truck allowed the firebox to be situated behind the high driving wheels, thereby permitting it to be both wide and deep.

When they saw how successful the design was in New Zealand, designers around the globe adopted it. Australia quickly got in on the act. In 1902 an order was placed with UK manufacturer Nasmyth, Wilson and Company, Vulcan Foundry and the North British Locomotive Company for 65 Pacifics, which became the Western Australia Government Railways E class. Another British builder, Kitson & Company, built the Karoo class for South Africa's Cape Government Railways in 1903. In the first half of the 20th century, Pacifics became the predominant type of steam haulage in North America. Between 1902 and 1930, around 6800 entered service in the US and Canada, with 45% constructed by the American Locomotive Company (ALCO) and 28% by Baldwin.

Two French prototypes designed by the Compagnie du chemin de fer de Paris à Orléans appeared in 1907, a few weeks before a German Pacific type that had come off the drawing board in 1905. The first British Pacific locomotive was built by the Great Western Railway in 1908 and named *The Great Bear*, the name of a constellation echoing the company's pioneer *North Star* locomotive of 1837.

Its designer, George Jackson Churchward, had already seen a member of his City 4-4-0 class, No. 3440 *City of Truro*, set an unofficial world steam speed record of 102.3mph on Wellington bank in Somerset on May 9, 1904. The City class was his first design as locomotive superintendent since he was appointed in 1902.

Churchward's great successes in locomotive design led to him being considered by many to be the most influential of all British railway engineers of the 20th century steam era. He made his name with types such as the superb Saint and Star express passenger 4-6-0s, which finally took the GWR out of the post-Isambard Kingdom Brunel era of locomotive design into the 'modern' age, breaking many moulds and setting new trends along the way.

In 1903, Britain's first 2-8-0, the 28XX class, appeared, followed by the UK's first 2-8-0 tank engines in the form of 4200 class built for the South Wales heavy coal traffic.

That year also saw the first of his hugely-successful large prairie tanks, the 3150 class, followed by a smaller version, the 45XX a year later. These were so successful, especially on branch line work all over the Swindon empire, that they saw service right up to the end of British Railways steam in the Sixties. In 1911, his multi-purpose 43XX 2-6-0s appeared.

Under Churchward, the GWR became renowned throughout the world for its engineering excellence, and just as he adopted ideas from abroad, notably the De Glehn compounds of France, there were many who tried to emulate him.

Churchward saw the soaring global successes of the Pacific type and decided to build one for the GWR. The company may have wanted the distinction of building the country's first 4-6-2, stealing a march on its competitors with a design that was being widely praised and adopted elsewhere. Churchward aimed to show it was possible to build a four-cylinder locomotive with 15in diameter cylinders which could be adequately fed by a standard GWR boiler, and it may have been that he saw a 4-6-2 as the logical next step in his ground-breaking work with 4-6-0 designs. Sadly, it was not a success.

No. 111 *The Great Bear*, outshopped from Swindon Works in February 1908, was restricted to being used primarily on the Paddington to Bristol line because of its high axle loading, which gave it a route availability of 'Special Red', although on one occasion it was recorded as having run to Wolverhampton.

Early on in its career, there were difficulties experienced with clearance on curves and also springing of the trailing wheels. Modifications also had to be made to the superheating of the boiler.

However, with Swindon Works diverting his attention to supplying military needs during the First World War, and Churchward's advances in the development of the 4-6-0s, *The Great Bear* became a project relegated to the back burner. By January 1924, it needed heavy repairs to its boiler after just 527,272 miles. As a result, it was dismantled and some of the parts were used by Churchward's successor Charles B Collett to build Castle class 4-6-0 No. 2975 *Viscount Churchill*.

Churchward, who had retired two years earlier, was clearly disappointed.

In 1922, he was told that a Pacific was to be built for the Great Northern Railway by its chief mechanical engineer, Nigel Gresley. He remarked: "What did that young man want to build it for? We could have sold him ours!"

Churchward never married and was a man who literally lived and died by steam. On December 19, 1933, at the age of 75, walking back to this Swindon home from a visit to the GWR works, he stepped across the main line tracks in thick fog. Despite suffering from poor eyesight and being hard of hearing, he stopped to examine a defective sleeper and was struck by the Paddington to Fishguard express, hauled by Castle class 4-6-0 No. 4085 *Berkeley Castle*, and killed.

THE EAST COAST MAIN LINE

The 393-mile East Coast Main Line is one of Britain's greatest railway arteries, linking London to Edinburgh, and roughly follows the route of the Great North Road, which in the 20th century became classified as the A1. It was built by not one but three separate companies, each with its own local interests and agenda, but each with the longer-term intention of linking up to form a through route between the two capital cities.

Six weeks before the Edinburgh & Glasgow Railway opened on February 21, 1842, its chairman John Learmonth met Edinburgh businessmen who wanted to build a line to the fishing port of Dunbar 30 miles to the east. Investors did not think this was a big enough 'catch', and so the scheme was beefed up to building the first railway across the border, to Berwick-upon-Tweed.

The scheme became the North British Railway, and opened amid huge public celebrations on June 18, 1846, with stagecoaches taking passengers onwards to Newcastle-on-Tyne. Because of the break in the journey, the North British was still struggling to take trade away from Leith to London passenger ships. The Newcastle & Berwick Railway meanwhile reached Berwick in March 1847, linking the port to the Brandling Junction Railway at Gateshead, but it was to be another 18 months before a temporary bridge was built to link it to the North British, allowing through running. The temporary bridge was superseded in July 1850 when Queen Victoria opened Robert Stephenson's magnificent 2162ft-long 124ft-high 28-arch brick-built Berwick viaduct or Royal Border Bridge across the River Tweed.

The York to Darlington section of the York & Newcastle Railway opened on March 30, 1841, but the company ran out of money, and so the Newcastle & Darlington Junction Railway completed the line to Newcastle, opening on June 19, 1844. Three years later, the Newcastle & Berwick Railway merged with the York & Newcastle Railway to become the York, Newcastle and Berwick Railway.

Meanwhile, work on the London & York Railway, quickly renamed the Great Northern Railway, began after its enabling Bill received Royal Assent on June 26, 1846. The Peterborough to Gainsborough section of a loop line was built first, before the intended GNR main line from Peterborough to Retford, with a connection from Lincoln to Retford via the Manchester Sheffield & Lincolnshire Railway, the first services over this section running on September 4, 1849.

The first section of track wholly owned by the GNR to be opened was the three-mile stretch from Doncaster to Askern Junction, on October 1, 1848. At Askern Junction, it was connected to the Lancashire & Yorkshire Railway line from Knottingley.

The loop line between Werrington, Peterborough and Lincoln opened on October 17 that year. The York & North Midland Railway reached agreement for the GNR to run trains over its line from Burton Salmon to York, and also over a new line from Knottingley to Burton Salmon, which opened in June 1850, in return for the GNR promising not to build a line from Selby to York.

So Peterborough became connected to York, Newcastle, Berwick and Edinburgh. Yet what about the ultimate destination – London? William Cubitt was appointed as engineer in chief for the GNR main line heading north from the capital, running from a temporary terminus at Maiden Lane north of the Regent's Canal to Peterborough via Biggleswade and Huntingdon. The line finally opened on August 7, 1850, just in time for the Great Exhibition of 1851.

The final link bringing the railway into Newcastle was Robert Stephenson's 133ft long six-span high level bowstring girder bridge which stands 131ft over the River Tyne at Newcastle, built between 1847-49. Its completion enabled trains to run from London to Edinburgh for the first time. Traffic began using it on August 15, 1849, with Queen Victoria performing the official opening on September 27 that year. At last, a new fast through route from London to Edinburgh was completed. And in August 1851, Victoria and Prince Albert journeyed from London to Scotland via the GNR.

However, the big drawback to the route was the missing section of proposed main line between Peterborough and Retford, avoiding the loop line that had been built first of all because it ran across flat fenland and did not need major engineering features. As it stood, the GNR route was slower than the Midland Railway's alternative.

William Cubitt's son Joseph became engineer-in-chief for the Peterborough to Retford line.

Huge local controversy arose as to whether the railway should pass through the great stagecoach town of Stamford in Lincolnshire, dividing local people, and in 1847 a parliamentary election was fought over the issue. The landowners who did not want the main line in the town won the day, and it ended up being served by a branch from Essendine, to Stamford's great commercial detriment, as the railway killed off the stagecoach trade virtually overnight.

Instead, the GNR main line bypassed Stamford, as it took a route from the edge of the Cambridgeshire fens north of Peterborough up a long ridge to Grantham. This gradient would immortalise the route within a century as the place where many speeds records would be set: Stoke Bank, the only major gradient on the line.

The line between Peterborough and Retford was finished in 1852 and the great terminus of King's Cross, designed by Lewis Cubitt, another member of the great family of civil engineers, opened on October 14 that year.

The GNR main line ended in a field at Shaftholme, a hamlet two miles north of Doncaster, where there was an end-on junction with the North Eastern Railway, an 1854 merger of the York, Newcastle & Berwick, the York & North Midland, the Leeds Northern and the Malton & Driffield Junction railways.

A direct line from Shaftholme Junction to York via Selby, opened in

January 1871, shortened the route somewhat – ending the running of express trains using the Askern route from Shaftholme to Knottingley, the Burton Salmon branch and the York & North Midland Railway line from Normanton to York. A new route from Durham to Newcastle was opened by the North Eastern Railway in 1872, shortening the distance and bypassing the section known as the Leamside line between Ferryhill and Pelaw. The Leamside line stayed open until 1991 however, being used as an alternative route and for stopping trains.

The North British, North Eastern and Great Northern railways did not amalgamate, but co-operated when it was in their best interests to do so. A primary example was the 1860 establishment of a fleet of special carriages for through running, known as the East Coast Joint Stock. In addition to the core King's Cross to Edinburgh route, the term East Coast Main Line is today taken to include its northern 'extension' via the Forth Bridge to Aberdeen.

THE RACES TO THE NORTH

The ECML runs on the opposite side of the country to the route from London to Glasgow, which was also built piecemeal by a series of companies and became known as the West Coast Main Line (WCML). Today, the latter is Britain's most important rail backbone in terms of population served, and also the busiest mixed-traffic railway route in Europe.

The first section of the WCML was opened in 1837. The Grand Junction Railway linking the Liverpool & Manchester Railway via Crewe to Birmingham was the world's first trunk railway, and in 1838 it was followed by the London & Birmingham Railway. The Trent Valley Railway, which built the West Midlands avoiding line between Rugby and Stafford, merged with it in 1846 to become the London & North Western railway.

The LNWR later absorbed three sections to the north, the North Union Railway from Wigan to Preston, the Lancaster & Preston Junction Railway and the Lancaster & Carlisle Railway. On September 10, 1847, the Caledonian Railway opened its main line from Carlisle to Beattock, extending it to Edinburgh in February 1848, which allowed through services to London from the 1850s onwards.

The LNWR marketed the entire route from Euston to Glasgow as the Premier Line, combining with the Caledonian to pool coaches as West Coast Joint Stock which made through running simpler. The line between London and Rugby was widened to four tracks in the 1870s to expand capacity with a new section, the Northampton Loop, opening in 1881.

In the great days of railway competition, it was inevitable that companies offering rival routes from London to Scotland would compete with each other both in terms of speed and comfort. Train travel had become an accepted part of everyday life by late Victorian times — it was no longer a novelty to complete a journey in hours that had once taken several days by stagecoach. The next step was to see just how quickly that journey could be undertaken, as advances in steam technology led to ever faster locomotives.

The result was what became known as the Races to the North, with fierce competition between the east and west coast routes. The first Race to the North took place in the summer of 1888, between daytime trains from London to Edinburgh. The second was in summer 1895, and involved night expresses running between London and Aberdeen, with the finishing post being Kinnaber Junction, 38 miles south of Aberdeen, where the Caledonian Railway and the North British Railway routes joined.

The Great Northern Railway's Stirling Single 4-2-2 No. 668 took the East Coast express 105.5 miles from King's Cross to Grantham in one hour 41 minutes with an average speed of 62.7mph on August 20, 1895. An engine change saw No. 775 take over, and complete the 82 miles to York in one hour 16 minutes, an average speed of 64.7mph. The overall trip was covered in six hours 19 minutes, at a speed of 63.5mph, while the extended run to Aberdeen, making a total of 523 miles, took eight hours 40 minutes, with an average speed of 60.4mph.

The LNWR responded two days later, and its Improved Precedent or 'Jumbo' express passenger 2-4-0 No. 790 *Hardwicke* took two hours and six minutes to cover the 141 miles from Crewe to Carlisle with an average speed of 67.1mph, setting a new speed record in the Races to the North.

One such race in 1895 saw both trains reach Kinnaber Junction at the same time. The Caledonian signalman sportingly decided to let the rival

North British train through, and it reached Aberdeen in eight hours 40 minutes from King's Cross, compared to the standard 12 hours 20 minutes before the races began. The following night, the West Coast Main Line companies responded by making an 'exhibition run' from Euston via Crewe to Aberdeen in eight hours 32 minutes.

The racing ended in the immediate aftermath of the Preston crash of July 13, 1896. A Euston to Glasgow train passed through the station at around 45mph, ignoring the 10mph speed limit on a tight curve, and left one passenger dead. A public outcry led to the focus shifting from speed to safety, and the rivals reached an agreement on speed limits, which were kept for more than three decades.

THE FUTURE KING OF SPEED

While the Races to the North gripped the public imagination in 1888 and 1895, the phrase 'you ain't seen nothing yet' quickly comes to mind from a historical perspective. Times would eventually change again, and there would come a day when even greater feats of steam and speed would inspire not just a British audience, but a global one too.

On the East Coast, it would be down to the design skills of one man – a railway engineering genius. Herbert Nigel Gresley.

Born on June 19, 1876, in Edinburgh, he was the son of the Reverend Nigel Gresley, rector of St Peter's church in Netherseal, then in Leicestershire but now in Derbyshire. He was not Scottish: his mother Joanna Beatrice, née Wilson, had merely visited the Scottish capital to see a gynaecologist. The Gresley family had roots in the Church Gresley locality in Derbyshire dating back to the Norman Conquest, when their ancestor came over from France with William I.

They descended from Nigel de Stafford, the son of Robert de Stafford, whose son Nigel took the name after the castle they held at Gresley. They held the 'manor of Drakelowe' from the conquest for nine centuries. Drakelow Hall, a large Elizabethan mansion, became the seat of the main line of the family, while a subsidiary branch had its seat at Netherseal Hall. The last of the Gresley family left Drakelow Hall in 1931, ending an unbroken succession of 28 generations who had lived there. Three years later, the house was knocked down to make way for Drakelow Power Station, which itself was later demolished. Netherseal Hall was knocked down in 1933.

Young Nigel, one of five children, first attended a preparatory school, Barham House, in Dane Road, St Leonards, Sussex, and then Marlborough College in Wiltshire where, as a member of B1 House, he developed his abilities for mechanical drawing and was top of the school in science. He distinguished himself in chemistry and German. One of his drawings, completed when he was just 14, today hangs in the Institution of Mechanical Engineers in London.

Rather than stay on into the sixth form, he opted for practical training and joined the LNWR. On October 17, 1893, he became a premier apprentice at Crewe Works, under the great 'King of Crewe', locomotive superintendent Francis Webb. In his first years, he would have undertaken mundane tasks in the engineering workshops, but still had in effect a ringside seat as the LNWR became engaged in the 1895 Races to the North.

Gresley then moved to the Lancashire & Yorkshire Railway works drawing office at Horwich, at the time overseen by chief mechanical engineer Sir John Aspinall. His leadership skills combined with his exceptional engineering skills saw him swiftly move up the ladder. While serving as locomotive foreman at Blackpool in 1899, he attended one of the Bolton Assembly Balls where he met his future wife Ethel Frances Fullagar, who lived at nearby St Anne's. They married in 1901.

Three years later, Gresley was promoted to the position of assistant superintendent of the carriage and wagon department of the L&YR. In 1905, the couple moved from Newton Heath in Manchester with their children Nigel and Violet to Milford, a house in Thorne Road, Doncaster, after becoming carriage and wagon superintendent at the age of 29.

Henry Alfred Ivatt, whose Atlantics had begun the GNR's big engine policy, retired from the position of GNR locomotive superintendent in 1911, and recommended Gresley to succeed him. Gresley, then 35, not only took over his position but also moved into his old home in Avenue House. Two more children were born at Doncaster, Roger and Marjorie, who later became a film actress.

The Gresleys gave their children a Christian upbringing, attending church on Sunday mornings and singing hymns around the family piano in the evening. Sometimes on Sundays, Nigel Gresley would give them a tour around Doncaster Works, showing them how locomotives were built.

They took family holidays at Braemar in Aberdeenshire, where Gresley indulged in his pastimes of shooting and fishing. They also visited seaside resorts including Sheringham, where he played golf. Gresley also kept dogs as pets, spaniels being his favourite breed.

Gresley sustained a severe injury while out shooting rooks during a stay at his mother's house in January 1910. While climbing a sloe hedge, a thorn stuck in his leg. It was difficult to remove and his brother Nigel tried to cut it out with a penknife he used for cleaning his pipe. The result was blood poisoning, and the local doctor thought that the leg might have to be amputated.

However, the GNR chairman heard about Gresley's plight and arranged for London specialist Sir Anthony Bowlley to visit him twice, such was the respect that the young superintendent had already earned. Bowlley was set to amputate the leg but decided as a last resort to try an old-fashioned remedy—leeches. They sucked out the poison and the leg was saved.

Gresley went with his wife on holiday to Bournemouth to recuperate and made a full recovery. During the First World War, Doncaster Works was largely turned over to munitions manufacture. Gresley became a lieutenant-colonel in the Engineer and Railway Staff Corps, RE (TF), being awarded the CBE in January 1920.

THE FIRST GRESLEY PACIFICS

Gresley's first locomotive design for the GNR was the H2 2-6-0 (LNER K1) in 1912. A conventional two-cylinder design, it was intended to speed up long-distance freight traffic. Six years later, he produced the Class O1 2-8-0s for heavy freight. These had three cylinders and for the first time incorporated Gresley's conjugated valve gear.

His first express engine was not a Pacific, but rather a H4 2-6-0 (LNER K3), built for sustained power rather than high speed. These locomotives had three cylinders and six small driving wheels, facilitating space for a large boiler. Indeed, the sheer size of the H4s raised many eyebrows in the railway industry and concerns were expressed over potential track damage due to their weight.

The GNR saw that while they were successful in their day, Ivatt's large-boilered 4-4-2s, the first of which, No. 251, appeared in 1902, were becoming unable to cope with the rise in traffic. Express trains were simply becoming too big for them. Gresley therefore drew up plans for an elongated version of the Ivatt Atlantic in 1915, with four cylinders, and experimented with a modified locomotive.

He was not happy with his design though, so looked further afield. In 1914, the Pennsylvania Railroad had introduced the first of 425 K4 Pacifics, a type which proved so successful that it lasted in traffic until finally ousted by diesels in 1957. The impact of the K4 type was so great that today it is officially acknowledged as the State Steam Locomotive of Pennsylvania.

Gresley sifted through reports on the K4s in detail and was clearly impressed. They inspired him to build a new type of modern steam locomotive for post-war Britain. He subsequently drew up plans for a pair of Pacifics to run on the East Coast Main Line as the forerunners of a new class to supersede Ivatt's Atlantics. Gresley's universal three-cylinder layout, which had been incorporated into two of his earlier designs, was again employed. The drive from all three cylinders was concentrated on the middle coupled axle.

The design incorporated the Gresley conjugated valve gear which enables a three-cylinder locomotive to operate with only the two sets of valve gear for the outside cylinders, and derives the valve motion for the inside cylinder from them by means of levers. Gresley's Pacific design would exploit the route's loading gauge to the full, with large boilers and wide fireboxes providing a large grate area. Heat transfer and the flow of gases were aided by a combustion chamber which extended forward from the firebox space into the boiler barrel.

Features in common with the Pennsylvania types were the downward profile towards the back of the firebox and the boiler tapering towards the front. However, the design did not utilise the flat-topped Belpaire firebox of the K4s, but adhered to GNR tradition in having a round-topped version.

The first of Gresley's Pacifics was No. 1470 *Great Northern*, named after the company, which entered traffic in 1922. It was followed by No. 1471 *Sir Frederick Banbury*. The GNR liked them and quickly ordered a production batch of ten. Meanwhile another of the East Coast companies, the North Eastern Railway, had begun building Pacifics. Sir Vincent Raven, its chief mechanical engineer, was decades ahead of his time when he began making plans to electrify the route from York to Newcastle, but was thwarted by the onset of a trade recession and industrial disputes in 1921.

In a swift change of heart, Darlington works produced a Pacific based on the earlier Z class Atlantic, with a longer boiler and wider firebox, but with its design otherwise firmly rooted in the past rather than the future.

CHAPTER 2

The 'Flying Scotsman' era

BRITAIN'S RAILWAYS were placed under state control during the First World War and the advantages of having them under one unitary authority became clear. There were calls to nationalise the railways after hostilities ended, but there were others who successfully argued that it was a move too far. History records that nationalisation would have to wait until January 1, 1948.

As a halfway house, the Liberal Government under David Lloyd George enacted The Railways Act 1921, also known as the Grouping, following proposals set out in a June 1920 White Paper, Outline of Proposals as to the Future Organisation of Transport Undertakings in Great Britain and their Relation to the State.

This facilitated the merger of most of the country's 120 railways into four main companies: the London, Midland & Scottish Railway, the Great Western Railway, the Southern Railway and the London & North Eastern Railway, at first known as the East Coast Group. One aim was to eliminate needless competition between routes that doubled up. It placed both east and west coast routes with a single company for each for the first time: the LMS taking control of the west and the LNER taking the east.

The Act took effect on January 1, 1923, but by that date most of the

28

mergers already had taken place, some from the previous year. In February 1923, *The Railway Magazine* called the new companies "The Big Four of the New Railway Era" and the term Big Four is still in use to this day.

There were three candidates for the post of chief mechanical engineer at the LNER: John Robinson, aged 66, from the Great Central Railway, Sir Vincent Raven, 63, from the North Eastern Railway, and Nigel Gresley, aged 46. The new LNER board was anxious to balance the appointment of officers between the new companies but Raven quit to join Metropolitan-Vickers anyway, leaving just Robinson and Gresley.

However, the LNER intended to introduce a retirement age of 65 and Robinson, who had been in charge of mechanical engineering at the GCR since 1900, was beyond it. A younger man was needed.

Robinson later claimed that he had been offered the job but declined it, instead recommending Gresley. Robinson was retained by the LNER for a year in a consultancy capacity and Gresley's appointment as CME was confirmed at a board meeting on February 23, 1923. He now found himself overseeing 30,000 staff and 12 workshops, along with 7400 engines, 21,000 carriages and 300,000 wagons.

The LNER continued with the building of Gresley's GNR Pacifics, but also pressed on with the Raven type, of which five were built. The first of these, No. 2400, later named *City of Newcastle*, appeared at the end of 1922 in North Eastern livery, but did not enter service until the LNER had taken over in January.

It was decided that only one of the two Pacific types would become the company's new standard express passenger locomotive. A series of test runs from London to Doncaster was organised to make the choice, using the North Eastern Railway's 1906-built dynamometer car which had state-of-the-art equipment for measuring speed over distance.

The Raven type fell short on fuel consumption and also demonstrated some mechanical shortcomings. So Gresley's A1s — the LNER designation of the class — won the day. The LNER was so impressed by them that it ordered another 40 to be built at Doncaster and 20 by North British. From the outset they had proved that they could haul bigger loads at faster speeds than Ivatt's Atlantics. During a test run, Great Northern took a

60-ton 20-coach train over the 105 miles from London to Grantham with an average speed of 51.8mph. The downside was that it consumed a huge amount of coal in the process.

A total of 31 Gresley A1s were built at Doncaster and another 20 by North British. One drawback of the A1s was that they had been designed to work on the GNR, which had no distances greater than 200 miles. Under the LNER, the distances they would need to run became significantly greater at a stroke.

A1 No. 1472 was outshopped in the early days of the LNER after being given a GNR number. It was renumbered 4472 and named *Flying Scotsman* for display in a Palace of Engineering at the British Empire Exhibition at Wembley in 1924 along with the GWR's first Castle 4-6-0, No. 4073 *Caerphilly Castle*. The GWR, with much justification, boasted that the Castle, with its 31,825lb tractive effort, was the most powerful locomotive in Britain.

The LNER and GWR held exchange trials between King's Cross and Doncaster and Paddington and Plymouth to see whether this claim was true. After two months, GWR No. 4079 *Pendennis Castle* won the day, climbing from King's Cross to Finsbury Park in less than six minutes, when running from King's Cross to Grantham, and King's Cross to Doncaster, beating Gresley's Pacifics including *Flying Scotsman*. The Castle was shown to have better coal and water economy.

Pendennis Castle attended the second Wembley Exhibition between May and October 1925 and was displayed next to *Flying Scotsman*, alongside a sign stating that No. 4079 was now the most powerful passenger express locomotive in Britain.

Beaten but undeterred, Gresley analysed the results of the trials. Experimental modifications were made to A1 No. 4477 *Gay Crusader*, based on GWR practice, in 1926. Its valve gear was adjusted to boost the performance of the Pacific 180psi boiler while using less coal and water, thereby making long-distance non-stop runs feasible.

The valve gear was afterwards redesigned and fitted to No. 2555 *Centenary* in 1927, and the rest of the class was similarly treated in the ensuing years.

A new improved class of Gresley Pacific appeared. These were the A3s, which incorporated both the results of the tests and the improvements made to the A1s. Another new feature was the change from right to left-hand drive, making it easier to sight signals. The first A3 was No. 2743 *Felstead*. It entered traffic in August 1928 with a 220psi boiler, increased superheat, and improved weight distribution. A total of 27 A3s were built new, but eventually all of the original A1s, including *Flying Scotsman*, were converted to A3s.

THE NEW 'SUPER A1' PACIFICS

It was with the launch of the famous LNER train the 'Flying Scotsman' that the advancements made by Gresley to his Pacifics hit home hard. The non-stop daily King's Cross to Edinburgh service was initially hauled by a pool of three A1s and two A3s, including *Flying Scotsman* with its modified valve gear, which pulled the first train on May 1, 1928.

The East Coast Main Line is often referred to as the route of the 'Flying Scotsman', a name which preceded the debut of No. 4472 by 50 years. After the Great Northern, North Eastern and North British railways set up the East Coast Joint Stock fleet of carriages, the GNR launched its 'Special Scotch Express' in 1862, with simultaneous departures at 10am from King's Cross and Edinburgh Waverley. By the time of the 1888 Race to the North, the speed had been cut from 10½ hours to 8½ hours. Around 1870, it unofficially became known as the 'Flying Scotsman'.

The LNER upgraded the train in 1924, officially renaming it the 'Flying Scotsman' for the first time, and named No. 4472 after it. Due to the agreement not to further reduce the eight hours 15 minutes time for the journey which had been brokered after the races to the North, the speed of the train would still be restricted.

Yet Gresley's modifications led to a reduction in coal consumption whereby the train could run non-stop with just one fully-laden coal tender. Ten special tenders were built for the 'Flying Scotsman' train with a coal capacity of nine tons instead of the usual eight, and corridors to allow relief footplate crews to take over halfway reduced fatigue levels.

The upgraded 'Scotsman' service included greater luxury for passengers, such as improved catering, and facilities including a barber's shop. The 1928 trip was the first non-stop run of a scheduled service over the whole 393 miles of the East Coast Main Line, but it was not a first between London and Scotland. Four days earlier, the rival LMS had run the Edinburgh portion of its 'Royal Scot' all 399.7 miles from Euston.

The old rivalry we saw in the previous chapter had been rekindled. The following year, No. 4472 was the centrepiece of the film The Flying Scotsman, which was set aboard the train and included several daring stunts performed while it was in motion. The speed limitation agreement was torn up in 1932, when the 'Flying Scotsman' was rescheduled to 7½ hours and six years later to seven hours 20 minutes. Spectacular ramifications were to follow.

Flying Scotsman's next golden and arguably greatest moment came on November 30, 1934. It was allocated to haul a test train between King's Cross and Leeds. The Down trip to Leeds had been completed in 152 minutes six seconds for the 185½ miles. It would be another 30 years before a similar timing was achieved on the King's Cross-Leeds run. On the way back, hauling six coaches weighing 208 tons, *Flying Scotsman* reached 100mph just outside Little Bytham on Stoke Bank in Lincolnshire. Furthermore, it held the speed for another 600 yards. And to cap it all, the speed was officially recorded, unlike that of GWR 4-4-0 *City of Truro* on its alleged 102.3mph run on Wellington Bank in 1904. It was the first time in the world that a steam locomotive had been officially recorded at 100mph — and Gresley's name was on the blueprint.

Driver William Sparshatt, 61, told onlookers before he left King's Cross that day: "If we hit anything today, we'll hit it hard."

The LNER publicity machine went into overdrive and for the railway the development of Gresley's Pacifics was the clear way ahead. LNER chief general manager Sir Ralph Wedgwood suggested that with an ordinary Pacific engine faster overall speeds could be maintained, with a train of much greater weight, capacity, and comfort.

A3 No. 2750 *Papyrus* turned in a series of outstanding performances on the ECML in March 1935. Running from King's Cross to Newcastle and back, the engine reached 108mph going down Stoke Bank while hauling

217 tons. It maintained a speed above 100mph for 12½ consecutive miles, the world record for a non-streamlined locomotive, shared with a French Chapelon Pacific.

Papyrus showed that it might even have been possible to work a four-hour service between King's Cross and Newcastle using A3 Pacifics, with a load of 200-220 tons.

However, a new breed of Pacific was by now being designed that would continue the progress towards cutting journey times on the East Coast route. Streamlining was being seen as the way forward.

Following the success of the *Papyrus* trials, Gresley was given the go-ahead to build the 'Silver Jubilee' streamlined trains. The aim was not only to reduce air resistance at high speed but also, for publicity purposes, to boost the glamour appeal of big express stream locomotives.

Modification of the front end of existing LNER Pacifics was considered as a cut-price option at the outset. Experiments at the National Physical Laboratory showed that streamlining an A3 could save more than 40hp at 60mph, rising to 97hp at 80mph and 138hp at 90mph, with an overall saving in power output of 10%. A new streamlined express passenger locomotive therefore would be the order of the day and it would be known as an A4.

Very similar in basic mechanical design to the A3, the A4 boilers had a higher pressure of 250psi and a reduced cylinder diameter to give greater power. However, it was to be the streamlined casing that would make the A4 one of the most distinctive and immediately recognisable locomotives on the planet.

CHAPTER 3

Racing inspiration

I F DIESEL traction and the motor car are considered superior to the steam locomotive, if only in terms of historical progression, then Gresley's streamlined A4s may be considered a glaring example of backward technology — because the inspiration for the air-smoothing shape of the A4s was a series of French high-speed diesel railcars!

Former Doncaster Works apprentice Walter Owen Bentley eventually became one of the biggest names in motor car manufacturing, his surname a byword for luxurious vehicles. He not only designed and raced cars but also was a designer of aero engines, founded Bentley Motors Ltd at Cricklewood and gained an MBE for his achievements.

However, Bentley began his career as an apprentice with the Great Northern Railway under Henry Alfred Ivatt at the age of 16 in 1905. There he worked with Gresley.

Much later, Bentley introduced Ivatt to the Italian-born French racing car designer and manufacturer Ettore Bugatti (born September 15, 1881), who had carried out extensive tests with pioneering wind tunnels to study the problem of aerodynamics — ultimately coming up with his most successful racing car, the Type 35.

Bugatti fell on hard times as a result of the Wall Street Crash in 1929. He had sold just three examples of his commercial model, the Type 41 Royale, and had to lay off half of his workforce. He desperately needed new ideas.

Gresley and his assistant Oliver V Bulleid often visited Bugatti in France. Both shared his interest in motor sport and became conversant with his streamlining techniques. In return, Bugatti sought the pair's advice on the prospect of building new high-speed trains for the French railways, which were also undergoing a severe downturn in trade. Like Michelin and Renault, other European motor manufacturers whose profits had suddenly nosedived, Bugatti turned to building railway vehicles and came up with several revolutionary designed for petrol railcars, with engines based on those of his Royale cars.

Bugatti was not a formally educated or qualified engineer, and yet came up with a remarkable product following two years of round-the-clock graft, producing his first sketch in October 1931. His railcars contained many new ideas, such as the chassis, body and the arrangement of the lightweight monocoque bogies with sophisticated systems for achieving a smooth, stable, quiet and comfortable ride. The cable operated twin shoe drum brakes were similar to Bugatti car brakes.

He built a prototype in spring 1933 and it was a rip-roaring success during main line trials. A production batch followed and several entered service between Paris and Deauville, reaching 113mph during tests.

Sadly, French safety restrictions inhibited his tests, allowing rival designs in Germany such as the 'Flying Hamburger', which hit 122mph, to go faster much sooner. Each railcar was equipped with four Bugatti Royale engines, with independent wheels fitted to one axle. The shape of the 'nose' of the unit made it more aerodynamic, and was similar to that of the much later French TGV locomotive. The design was striking in the extreme by the standards of the day, with smoothly-rounded corners and wedge-shaped front and back ends.

The Bugatti railcars were built as single, double or triple 'car' units with either two or four 12.7 litre petrol engines centrally mounted in one of the cars. Each car was mounted on a pair of eight-wheel bogies and the linked engines were arranged to drive two or four of the eight axles via drive shafts with hydraulic clutches and reversing gears. This modular system of powered and trailer cars could be arranged in various combinations to suit the different needs of the French railway companies, from the smallest 36 seater to the triple-set 144-seat train.

The fastest and most luxurious Bugatti railcar was *Presidential*, so named after its inaugural trip on the Paris-Chartres line carrying the President of the Republic, Albert Lebrun. It had four engines producing 800hp in a double set with 48 seats and it too reached 122mph in 1934, setting a new world railway speed record.

These railcars were highly successful, being light, clean and comfortable as compared with steam powered rolling stock. Their chief asset was speed and the ability to drastically reduce long distance journey times.

With a few years, Bugatti had turned his fortunes around through railcars, and eventually had more than 100 vehicles running in France. Interest came from far and wide and among his admirers was Gresley, who took on board many of his streamlining ideas when designed his A4s. Gresley was concerned with steam from the chimney blocking the driver's view — dangerous at high speed, especially as in a steam engine the only vision of the road ahead was through a small observation window.

He had looked at experimental designs old and new in the USA and Germany, but eventually decided that Bugatti's streamlining techniques were the best. Bugatti's horizontal wedge shape not only cut wind resistance and avoided disturbance to slower passing trains, but also lifted the smoke clear of the engine on most occasions.

Gresley tested Bugatti's designs at the National Railway Physical Laboratory in Teddington, and the City and Guilds Engineering College in London, and found them to be superior. Bugatti entertained Gresley and Bulleid during a trip on one of his railcars between Paris and Le Havre and Paris and Deauville in 1933. Gresley was less than impressed on this occasion however, and found the ride bumpy at more than 80mph — a complaint often made about these railcars.

Yet many of Bugatti's streamlining ideas were incorporated into the A4, a locomotive designed to show that there was still very much a place for steam in a world which one day might be dominated by diesel and electric power.

Ettore Bugatti died in Paris in August 1947 — outliving Gresley by six years — and was buried in the family plot in Dorlisheim near Molsheim. As petrol became more expensive after the Second World War, Bugatti railcars, which were heavy on fuel, were phased out.

THE 'FLYING HAMBURGER'

In Germany, there were fewer track speed safety restrictions than in France when testing new prototypes on the main line. In the wake of Adolf Hitler's rise to power, great emphasis was placed on modernising the Reichsbahn as a means of alleviating the unemployment that had dogged the Weimar Republic. This not only boosted the nation's industry but also led to the creation of prestige projects that the whole world would admire. One such project was the 'Flying Hamburger', correctly termed the Deutsche Reichsbahn-Gesellschaft Class SVT 877 'Hamburg Flyer'.

This streamlined two-car railcar set was Germany's first high-speed diesel-electric train, and staked its claim to being the fastest regular railway connection in the world in its day. It was ordered in 1932 from Waggon- und Maschinenbau AG Görlitz and entered service the following year. Wind tunnel experiments were also used to determine the shape of the 'Flying Hamburger', building on the development of the high-speed inter-urban railcar 'Bullet' two years before.

The train initially had 98 seats in two saloon coaches and a four-seat buffet. Each of the two coaches had a 12-cylinder Maybach diesel engine, with a direct current generator coupled to it, driving a Tatzlager-traction motor. The two engines developed a combined power of 604kW. The set had a pneumatic brake and an electromagnetic rail brake. At 99mph it needed 2600ft of track to come to a halt.

Beginning on May 15, 1933, the train ran regularly between Berlin (Lehrter Bahnhof) and Hamburg's central station, covering the 178 miles in 138 minutes — an astonishing average speed of 77.4mph. Such a performance would not be equalled until 64 years later, when Deutsche Bahn began to use InterCityExpress trains between the two cities in May 1997.

Seats on the 'Flying Hamburger' were so popular that they had to be booked several weeks before. Gresley watched proceedings from afar and discussed events in Germany with his friend, the future Prime Minister Winston Churchill. In May 1933, Gresley and Bulleid gained approval from the LNER board to see the 'Flying Hamburger' for themselves. If it was as good as the Germans wanted everyone to believe, the LNER might test a set in the UK.

A month after the 'Hamburger' was launched, LNER officials including Bulleid visited Berlin to take a trip on it. While the party was made very welcome, their German hosts declined to let them see maintenance operations and refused to discuss technical details. Bulleid managed to discover that there had been many problems with the set, reported while it was being tested in the Netherlands. Regardless, the LNER contingent reported back that they had been impressed.

Gresley himself visited Germany in 1934 to see if the 'Flying Hamburger' might be suitable for the East Coast Main Line. One big drawback was the cramped passenger compartments. Gresley, quite rightly, realised that passengers would not be prepared to stand being cooped up in them for a King's Cross to Edinburgh journey lasting several hours.

He remained convinced that his Pacifics could do the job better, but nonetheless asked the Germans to quote on delivering a three-car set for use between King's Cross and Newcastle, a journey of four hours. However, the Germans could not promise to beat this time for the 268-mile trip. Nor could hot meals be served to passengers — a big minus for a company like the LNER which boasted about its high quality service to passengers.

In many ways, the 'Flying Hamburger' paved a way ahead for the future of railways, and was the prototype for the later German Class SVT 137 sets. However, in its day, it encouraged engineers on both sides of the North Sea to develop even faster steam locomotives to show that they could do the job just as well.

CHAPTER 4

Silver Link, the 'Silver Jubilee' and the 'Coronation'

S ILVER LINK was the first of Nigel Gresley's A4s. Its appearance was startling and those who instinctively show disdain to anything new or radically different would have been horrified, especially those who preferred the conventional outline of a steam locomotive.

The 'Silver Jubilee' was so named because it was built in 1935, the year of King George V's Silver Jubilee. It comprised seven coaches: two twin-set articulated coaches and one triple-set. Not only were the A4s which were designed to pull it streamlined, but the coaches were too. Painted silver throughout, the train was a monument to the art deco styling of the era.

It ran between King's Cross and Newcastle at an average speed of 67mph, taking four hours to complete the journey. The timing of the 'Silver Jubilee' required speeds of 70 to 75mph to be sustained up the 1-in-200 gradients like Stoke Bank, with a 235 ton load behind the tender. On the level, the timings called for sustained speeds of 85 to 90mph. The A4s would be working their hardest at 75mph and above, the opposite of normal conditions on the heavy trains.

Gresley made several changes from the A3 design for the A4s. The exhaust was made freer by the use of 9in diameter piston valves, as opposed to the previous 8in, and the pressure drop between the boiler and the steam chest was virtually eliminated by streamlined passages, as well as by the increased fluidity of the steam itself, due to the higher boiler pressure of 250lb per sq in and a higher degree of superheat.

The softer blast resulting from the freer exhaust would have created less draught in the firebox had the A3 boiler been retained, with, possibly, an adverse effect upon the steaming; so with the A4s the boiler barrel was shortened from 19ft to 18ft, and the consequent reduction in tube heating surface was compensated for by the use of a combustion chamber. The cylinders of the A4s were slightly smaller, with an 18½in diameter against 19in.

A trial run was held over the East Coast Main Line on September 27, 1935, with an A4 called *Silver Link*. The engine, then just three weeks out of Doncaster Works, twice reached 112½mph, at Arlesey and Sandy, and maintained an average of 100mph for 43 consecutive miles. The press were invited aboard to see for themselves just what an A4 Pacific could do, and they were not disappointed.

Three days later, the 'Silver Jubilee' was launched, and was an overnight success. *Silver Link* completed the 536½-mile daily return journey for its first 13 trips without any serious mechanical problems, although on more than one occasion while shedded overnight at Gateshead, the brick arch needed partial rebuilding.

The 'Silver Jubilee' was a new standard for speed in Britain. In *The Railway Magazine* of November 1935, railway author Cecil J Allen wrote: "To those of us who for many years past have striven to advance the cause of high speed as one of the chief competitive weapons that railways possess in popularising their passenger travel, the introduction of the 'Silver Jubilee' express by the London & North Eastern Railway marks the most important and decisive step that has yet been taken in this direction in Great Britain.

"The service is operated by the first locomotive and train which have been built in this country expressly for high-speed running. The cuts of 67 minutes down and 66 minutes up that it makes below the best previously existing all-the-year-round timings on the London-Newcastle service (a reduction of 22%) in themselves embody a record long-distance acceleration for this country.

"The 'Silver Jubilee' is also notable as expressing the determination of the LNER, and of Mr H N Gresley, the designer, in particular, to exploit to the full the speed possibilities of steam traction before seeking higher speeds with diesel propulsion, following the lead already given by American railways, such as the Chicago, Milwaukee, St Paul & Pacific with its steam-hauled Hiawatha.

"Few of those who travelled on the trial run of September 27 are ever likely to forget their impressions on that most amazing journey. That an engine whose existence on rails had been barely three weeks could forthwith, on its first serious trial, smash almost every high speed railway record that has ever been made public, was astonishing enough. More so still, probably, is the fact that three days later the same engine went into regular service, and, as *Quicksilver* – the second engine of the class – had not then been run in, sustained for a fortnight the whole brunt of the new schedule, making two non-stop runs of 232.3 miles every day at average speeds of over 70mph. It travelled in all 536.3 miles every day, in rough weather conditions, to time on a schedule very much faster than anything which had been previously in force over this route, and all without heating, mechanical failure or trouble of any kind.

"Locomotive history probably has no parallel to such a feat as this. It affords unbounded credit to the designing genius of Mr H N Gresley and his staff, to the quality of workmanship at Doncaster Works, and to the expert handling of the new machine by the four King's Cross engine crews concerned."

Four streamlined Pacifics were built for the Silver Jubilee service, three of which, *Silver Link*, No. 2510 *Quicksilver* and No. 2512 *Silver Fox* were stationed at King's Cross. The fourth, No. 2511 *Silver King*, was the spare engine and allocated to Gateshead shed, where it acted as pilot for the Up 'Jubilee', afterwards usually operating the Newcastle-Edinburgh-York-Newcastle turn beginning with the 11.10am non-stop express to Edinburgh.

In 1936, the LNER added a dynamometer car to the 'Silver Jubilee', increasing the load to 254 tons during trial runs between Newcastle and King's Cross, and Newcastle and Edinburgh.

The first run, on August 27, 1936, saw *Silver Fox* achieve 113mph while going down Stoke Bank. On the northbound run the same day, *Silver Link* covered 15.3 miles from Tallington up to Stoke Summit at an average of 82.7mph, with the locomotive working on 18% cut-off and a wide-open regulator. These service trains were also trials to measure water and coal consumption, and to beat *Silver Link's* 112mph.

The LNER did not tell driver George Haygreen beforehand that a record was to be attempted on Stoke Bank. Accordingly, he had neither sufficient speed on the run up the gradient, nor enough boiler pressure in reserve. Despite these factors, *Silver Link* still set a new British record for a steam train in ordinary service carrying fare-paying passengers. As a result of the achievements of *Silver Link* and *Silver Fox*, it was established that an A4 had enough power to haul a 10-coach train at speed.

The A4s kept time brilliantly and rarely had to exceed 90mph to keep to their schedules. On a handful of occasions an 'ordinary' engine, an A3 or an Atlantic, might substitute for an A4 on the train. On a trip between Newcastle and Edinburgh, No. 2511 *Silver King* made an exceptional climb of the 1-in-96 Cockburnspath Bank, holding a speed of 68mph.

In January 1937, a fifth A4 appeared in No. 4482 *Golden Eagle*. It was the first in a new batch for use on both the fastest ordinary expresses and the new 'Coronation' express from King's Cross to Waverley, which commemorated the ascension to the throne of King George VI and was based on the art deco 'Silver Jubilee' but with a blue two-tone livery. It comprised four sets of two-car articulated units, with a special 'Beavertail' observation car designed with sloping back added to the rear during the summer months.

The A4s allocated to the 'Coronation' were painted in a special garter blue livery with red wheels. This later became standard for the class. The 'Coronation' began running from July 4, 1937, departing King's Cross at 4pm and arriving at 10pm. The addition of even more luxury carriages brought the weight of the train up to 312 tons, as opposed to the 220 tons of the

'Silver Jubilee'. Hauling it, the A4s had to work harder, while making the six-hour trip without being changed. Coal consumption could soar to the point where nearly all nine tons in the tender would be used.

The train ran until four days before the Second World War, during which the coaches were stored. Streamlined services ended on August 31, 1939, due to the enactment of the Emergency Powers (Defence) Act 1939.

From September 27, 1937, the LNER introduced a streamlined service for Leeds and Bradford, the 'West Riding Limited', with the carriages painted in the same blue livery as the 'Coronation'. The LNER aimed to attract business from the local woollen trade, and two new A4s were named accordingly. No. 4495 *Great Snipe* became *Golden Fleece*, while No. 4496 was named *Golden Shuttle* (renamed in 1946 as *Dwight D. Eisenhower*). In 1937, King George VI knighted Gresley for his services to the rail industry as chief mechanical engineer of the LNER.

LNER A4 PACIFICS: THE COMPLETE LIST IN ORDER OF BUILDING

LNER No.	Original name	Renaming	BR No.	Withdrawn
2509	Silver Link		60014	1962
2510	Quicksilver		60015	1963
2511	Silver King		60016	1965
2512	Silver Fox		60017	1963
4482	Golden Eagle		60023	1964
4483	Kingfisher		60024	1966
4484	Falcon		60025	1964
4485	Kestrel	Miles Beevor	60026	1965
4486	Merlin		60027	1965
4487	Sea Eagle	Walter K Whigham	60028	1962
4488	Osprey	Union of South Africa	60009	1966
4489	Woodcock	Dominion of Canada	60010	1965
4490	Empire of India		60011	1964
4491	Commonwealth of Australia		60012	1964
4492	Dominion of New Zealand		60013	1963
4493	Woodcock		60029	1963
4494	Osprey	Andrew K. McCosh	60003	1962
4495	Great Snipe	Golden Fleece	60030	1962
4496	Golden Shuttle	Dwight D. Eisenhower	60008	1963
4497	Golden Plover		60031	1965
4498	Sir Nigel Gresley		60007	1966
4462	Great Snipe	William Whitelaw	60004	1966
4463	Sparrow Hawk		60018	1963
4464	Bittern		60019	1966
4465	Guillemot		60020	1964
4466	Herring Gull	Sir Ralph Wedgwood	60006	1965
4467	Wild Swan		60021	1963
4468	Mallard		60022	1963
4469	Gadwall	Sir Ralph Wedgwood		1942
4499	Pochard	Sir Murrough Wilson	60002	1964
4500	Garganey	Sir Ronald Matthews	60001	1964
4900	Gannet		60032	1963
4901	Capercaillie	Sir Charles Newton	60005	1964
4902	Seagull		60033	1962
4903	Peregrine	Lord Faringdon	60034	1966

CHAPTER 5

Racing again with a vengeance: the streamlined rivals

ONE OF the biggest problems inherent in the Grouping of 1923 is that substantial companies with their own distinct ideologies were suddenly yanked together with odd bedfellows for geographical reasons into one of the new 'Big Four' companies, with an internal culture clash the inevitable outcome.

It was not so much of a problem with the GWR, as it retained its pre-Grouping identity and effectively absorbed the smaller companies it 'merged' with. However, with the other three, the Grouping was not always a marriage made in heaven.

The biggest difficulty with the formation of the new London Midland & Scottish Railway was the bringing together of old rivals the London & North Western and Midland railways. Accordingly, the first few years of the LMS were dogged by infighting. Higher management posts became filled by Midland men who would not budge from their beliefs that the Derby approach was the best, and adopted the Midland's crimson lake livery as standard for the whole of the 'Big Four' company. In the field of locomotive power, the LNWR and Midland ways of thinking were worlds apart.

The Crewe contingent followed a 'raw power' approach, with big engines to haul heavy trains over long distances, such as the West Coast Main Line and the upland country north of Manchester. The Midland, however, with its much shallower gradients, notoriously had a 'little engine' policy, with smart, polished, immaculately-turned out smaller locomotives which often had to double head to haul average heavy loads, wasting resources.

At the start, the LMS found itself desperately short of big engines, with even LNWR types struggling to haul the Anglo-Scottish expresses on their own. Despite this problem, the locomotive department, dominated by Derby men, continued to turn out large numbers of smaller engines like Class 2P 4-4-0s, and three-cylinder compounds, which was not exactly what was needed.

The LMS launched its new 15 coach 'Royal Scot' train from Euston to Glasgow in summer 1927. It needed to be hauled by an LNWR Claughton assisted by a George the Fifth or Precursor south of Carnforth, and by a pair of new compounds over Shap summit. It was clear that what was needed was one locomotive that could do it all by itself.

Sir Henry Fowler, former chief mechanical engineer of the Midland Railway, had been responsible for the small engine policy. He was promoted to the same position with the LMS in 1925, and a year later, began designing a compound Pacific express passenger locomotive, but failed to get support. Instead, LMS management looked to Charles Collett's world-beating GWR Castle class 4-6-0s, and borrowed No. 5000 *Launceston Castle* for a month, running it between Euston and Carlisle. The LMS was so impressed that it asked the GWR to build it a batch of Castles, but was turned down. Neither would the GWR board agree to allowing the LMS to borrow a full set of Castle drawings.

The LMS replaced Fowler's Pacific scheme with what they dubbed an 'Improved Castle,' which also drew much from the Southern Railway's Lord Nelson 4-6-0s and Fowler's new 2-6-4 tank engines. The net result was the Royal Scot class of 4-6-0s, true classics that appeared in 1927 and were capable of hauling 420-ton top LMS expresses on their own over Beattock and Shap.

Undaunted, the LMS finally acquired GWR Castle expertise and knowledge in the form of Swindon Works manager William Stanier, who was headhunted to become chief mechanical engineer in 1931, a year after Fowler had been shunted aside. Stanier knew the GWR locomotive types inside out, and the LMS tasked him to build it new modern powerful engines too.

One of his most successful types of all was the 'Black Five' mixed traffic 4-6-0, of which 842 were built — these being considered by many as the best all-round steam engines ever to run in the UK. The freight version was the Stanier 8F 2-8-0s, of which 852 were built.

However, what concern us here are big glamorous locomotives capable of equalling and bettering what was being developed by the LNER on the East Coast line. When Stanier took over, the LMS had no locomotive in its stable which had the ability to haul a 500 ton express on its own all 401 miles from Euston to Glasgow. Stanier built three prototype Pacifics, beginning with No. 6200 *The Princess Royal*, outshopped on June 27, 1933, and No. 6201 *Princess Elizabeth*. Their success led to batches being built. They were designed to haul the 'Royal Scot' train; the name for the class was chosen because Mary, the Princess Royal, was the Commander-in-Chief of the Royal Scots.

At this point in time, Britain was battling its way out of the Great Depression, and railway companies needed to increase their revenues. Far from eliminating rivalry and 'doubling up' of routes, the Grouping resulted in a return to the Races to the North, as the old 1896 agreements about limiting speeds were dropped. With effective motive power on the 'Royal Scot', the LMS was now able to compete with the LNER's 'Flying Scotsman' on London to Scotland traffic.

When the LNER's second streamlined train, the 'Coronation', was introduced, it brought the King's Cross to Edinburgh time down to six hours, with one stop. The LMS responded with plans for its own six-hour non-stop service from London to Glasgow, and arranged a trial run. Tom Clark, the senior driver from Crewe North shed, was chosen, with fireman Charles Fleet and passed fireman Albert Shaw assisting on a test train from Euston to Glasgow Central behind No. 6201.

On November 16, 1936, Clark took the train from Euston to Glasgow Central in five hours 53 minutes 38 seconds, and showed that the LNER had not won the day yet. The following day they made the return non-stop journey in five hours 44 minutes 14 seconds, at an average speed of 69mph, with an average load of 240 tons.

Front page newspaper headlines proclaimed "401 Miles Non Stop" and "London-Glasgow Under 6 Hours" — hailing the crew as national heroes.

Yet Stanier knew he had to do more to equal Gresley's A4s. His next and arguably greatest design was also a streamliner, in the form of the Princess Coronation Pacific; an enlarged version of the Princess Royal. The 38 examples made were the most powerful passenger steam locomotives ever built for use in Britain, capable of producing 3300hp.

The first five, Nos. 6220-4, were streamlined in a distinctive bulbous art deco air-smoothed casing and painted Caledonian Railway blue with silver horizontal lines to match the new LMS 'Coronation Scot' train. The tenders were each fitted with a steam-operated coal pusher to bring the coal down to the firing plate as an aid to the firemen.

The first of the new Pacifics was No. 6220 *Coronation*, and the LMS called on Tom Clark to drive it on June 29, 1937, in a bid to snatch back the world steam speed record from the LNER, a week before the 'Coronation Scot' was due to be launched. Clark covered the 158 miles from Euston to Crewe in two hours nine minutes 45 seconds, recapturing the record with a top speed of 114mph, claimed just south of Crewe, although many believe that 113mph was nearer the mark.

The trip is often remembered for Clark taking a 20mph restriction on a reverse curve at Crewe at 50mph, showing that the locomotive and train could handle it, and speeding at 60-70mph when it approached the Crewe platform signal, sent the crockery in the dining car crashing to the floor. He brought the 2700 ton train to a standstill at Crewe, with the engine and coaches still on the track.

The return trip from Crewe back to Euston took 119 minutes, an average of 79.7mph, one of the fastest ever recorded in Britain. The main highlight was the 69.9 miles from Walton to Willesden Junction, which took 47 minutes one second at an average of 89.3mph, with a maximum speed of 100mph at Castlethorpe water troughs. The train arrived at Euston 16 minutes ahead of schedule. As a result, the fastest start-to-stop runs of over 100 and 150 miles were claimed by the LMS.

The next day, A4 Pacific No. 4489 *Dominion of Canada* hauled the trial run of the LNER's 'Coronation', its version of the 'Coronation Scot'. With a heavier train of 320 tons, No. 4489 did not reach 113-4mph, but hit 109.5mph down Stoke Bank, and impressed with an 80.9mph climb from Arlesey to Stevenage.

On July 12, 1937, less than a month after claiming the world speed record, Clark drove the Royal Train from Crewe to Euston, where King George VI presented him with an OBE for his record runs to and from Glasgow the year before. The incident of the broken crockery led the LMS and LNER to make a truce, agreeing that no more record-breaking runs for publicity purposes should be held.

It would not, however, be the final word on the world steam speed record.

CHAPTER 6

The common enemy

I N THE wake of the successful demonstration of the 'Flying Hamburger'
high-speed diesel railcar set, Nigel Gresley and the LNER were not
alone in their belief that steam could still do the job just as well.

Neither was the LMS the only source of competition with regard to
speed records. The Germans too believed that steam's finest hour was still
to come. The Borsig locomotive works applied experimental streamlining
to a Deutsche Reichsbahn-Gesellschaft's Class 03 Pacific, a type built
for express passenger work between 1930-38, and carried out a series of
test runs.

Using the data from the experiments, three giant streamlined 4-6-4s
86ft 2in long were built as Germany's Class 05. These included the similar
Nos. 05001 and 05002, and No. 05003, which ran the cab at the front,
giving a clear view of the road ahead, as in a modern diesel or electric
locomotive. The latter was later rebuilt and lost the cab forward design.
Nos. 05001 and 05002 were used for test runs, mainly on trips between
Hamburg and Berlin from 1935-36.

On June 7, 1935, No. 05002 reached a top speed of 119.1mph near Berlin.
It made a further six test runs, reaching 110mph with trains weighing up
to 250 tons. Its crowning moment of glory came on May 11, 1936, when it

hauled a 194 ton train on the Berlin to Hamburg line, reaching 124mph, the locomotive having produced 2535kW of power. It was a new world record, beating anything that Gresley or Stanier had done up to then.

However, this was no ordinary test run, and neither was the speed record intentional. German railway officials had become concerned at Adolf Hitler's support for road transport since the Nazi party came to power in 1933. Days after becoming chancellor, Hitler announced a major autobahn construction project which Fritz Todt, the inspector general of German Road Construction, was appointed to oversee, with 130,000 workers given jobs and another 270,000 employed in the supply chain. It was indeed a major investment in the Germany economy coming after the Great Depression and the 'wheelbarrow money' period of the Weimar Republic.

The Nazi propaganda ministry turned the building of the autobahns into a significant publicity exercise that attracted international attention. They were the first limited-access, high-speed road network in the world, with the first section from Frankfurt-am-Main to Darmstadt opening in 1935.

Just as Britain's railways were to lose out big time to road competition, leading to mass closures before, during and after the Beeching era, so Deutsche Reichsbahn-Gesellschaft saw a major threat to its system emerging.

The railway's top brass needed to show the Nazi hierarchy that their system still had much to offer. A special three-leg train was arranged for party leaders, to show them that railways were still ahead of the game. The final leg saw No. 05002 take the train from Berlin to Hamburg. It ran smoothly, until, frustratingly, a series of red signals slowed it down.

Railway officials feared that the irritation of the VIP guests on board would turn to anger and contempt and the footplate crew were told to throw caution to the winds and let fly all the way back to Hamburg. They did so, and inadvertently set the new world record. The special train covered the 70.1 miles from Wittenberge to a signal stop before Berlin-Spandau in 48 min 32 seconds, at an average start-stop speed of 86.66mph.

Included in that party of guests were two individuals whose names would within a few years become a byword for the worst that humanity had — or ever will have — to offer the world: Heinrich Himmler and Reinhard Heydrich. Not bothered about steam records, the pair would concoct another very different purpose for the railways — not only of Germany but of all continental Europe. Following Germany's invasion of the Soviet Union in 1941 under Operation Barbarossa, extermination camps were set up in the newly-conquered territories of the east, where, out of sight of the ordinary Germany public, millions of innocent people who did not fit in with Nazi master race ideology would be murdered on an industrial scale, often within hours of their arrival.

Rail transport made mass killings on such an industrial scale possible, and one name emerged as the hub of Himmler and Heydrich's rail network of evil: Auschwitz. Deutsche Bundesbahn (German Federal Railway), the 1949 successor to Deutsche Reichsbahn-Gesellschaft, considered scrapping the then de-streamlined Class 05s after the war, but returned No. 05003 to traffic in 1950, and the other two in 1951, but with a lower power output. They mainly headed the FD long distance express trains Hanseat and Domspatz on the 437-mile Hamburg-Cologne-Frankfurt run with a regular top speed of 87mph. It was the longest run with steam traction on the DB network.

Ousted by Class V200 diesel hydraulics in 1958, No. 05001 was preserved at the DB museum in Nuremberg, where it can be seen today in its streamlined form with its original red livery. The other two including the record breaking No. 05002 were scrapped in 1960.

CHAPTER 7

The shining moment

NIGEL GRESLEY and the LNER not only wanted to beat their rivals Stanier and the LMS, but were also bent on reclaiming the world steam speed crown. Both would reap rich dividends in terms of publicity.

The problem with running faster and faster is that braking distance becomes longer; first and foremost, braking systems had to be improved. Furthermore, signalling systems needed to be improved, and at the time the East Coast Main Line did not have automatic signalling. Gresley looked at the Westinghouse system used by his rival the LMS and arranged a series of trials which involved rapid acceleration, followed by the brake test.

The locomotive selected for the tests would be No. 4468 *Mallard*, which seemed to have been given preferential treatment from the time it was being built at Doncaster. Indeed, there has been speculation that *Mallard* was named after one of the species of wild ducks that lived in the medieval moat around Salisbury Hall near London Colney in Hertfordshire, which Gresley leased after his wife's death in 1929 at the age of 54.

Appearing on LNER order number EO342 in November 1936, *Mallard* cost £8500 to build and was given the Doncaster Works number 1870. It received all the latest modifications afforded to class members and was the first of the class to be fitted with the Kylchap double chimney and blastpipe — as earlier tested on A3 No. 2751 *Humorist* and which allowed the smoke to be distributed more easily — and then the new Westinghouse QSA (Quick Service Application) brake valves.

Further improvements to the streamlined shape of the A4 were made in order to minimise the dispersal of smoke from the chimney at the front of the locomotive. Gresley's staff were working with the National Physical Laboratory at Teddington using a 1:12 scale model of *Mallard* and, after much trial and error, hit upon a simple solution purely by chance. A minor indentation in the Plasticine at the rear of the chimney on the model sent the smoke clear of the engine. Needless to say, Gresley was delighted.

Despite his health failing and having already achieved more than most chief mechanical engineers, Gresley was determined to try for the world record.

Mallard emerged from Doncaster Works on March 3, 1938, and Gresley asked Norman Newsome, his technical assistant, for carriages and wagons to organise a special brake test on the East Coast Main Line. Then Gresley, 62 at the time, set about selecting the right men for the job on the footplate.

He chose Joseph 'Joe' Duddington as the driver. Duddington, who was based in Doncaster, was not only renowned for pushing engines hard, but had also taken a shine to *Mallard* and had looked after it ever since it left the works. He had joined the Great Northern Railway in March 1895 at the age of 18 and was passed for firemen's duties three years later.

He worked his way up through the links to become a main line driver in March 1913 and had vast experience with the top East Coast locomotives in the period that Henry A Ivatt's Atlantics gave way to Gresley's Pacifics. Against Duddington was his age, 61, but Gresley knew only too well an important factor so often overlooked in many walks of life today — that youth cannot beat experience. Fireman Thomas Bray had been with *Mallard* as long as Duddington and knew how to get the best out of an A4.

In late June, Duddington and Bray were told by Gresley's King's Cross office to prepare themselves for a special mission, but were not told exactly what, as it was top secret. However, there had been much speculation on the LNER rumour mill for several weeks. Newsome, who had been told by Gresley that he hoped to beat the 114mph British record set by the LMS, arranged for the special test to be undertaken on Sunday, July 3.

Three twin-car sets from the 'Coronation' stock, along with the luxurious 1906-built North Eastern Railway teak dynamometer car No. 902502, were arranged. The weight of the train was 240 tons. Gresley himself chose *Mallard* and the Doncaster footplate crew rather than one of its King's Cross counterparts. In the run-up to the tests, he told his deputy Douglas Edge what the aim of the brake tests was.

The Westinghouse braking team arrived at Wood Green waterworks sidings in north London on July 3 to find a pristine *Mallard*, which had arrived at King's Cross the day before, coupled to the dynamometer car. Gresley had to miss the big day because he was ill at home, so standing in for him was Edge. Newsome was also on board, as was Bernard Atkinson from the locomotive running department and Eric Bannister, who had helped find the solution to the chimney problem at the testing laboratory.

Again, the true purpose of the trip was not revealed to the footplate crew, inspector Sam Jenkins or the Westinghouse team until the train had left Wood Green at 11.46am. The outward journey involved a series of ordinary brake tests between 90-100mph, with Denis Carling, the LNER test inspector, overseeing the recording in the dynamometer car. The run ended as intended at Barkston, a few miles north of Grantham in Lincolnshire, where the branch to Sleaford and Boston left the main line where the locomotive and dynamometer car were turned on the triangle.

It had been worked out that a good run south from Barkston would give the A4 the chance to climb Stoke Bank at speed, with the record being attempted on the downward grade.

The train arrived at Barkston at 2.49pm before those on board had lunch in the restaurant car. Sam Jenkins then tested a special intercom which had been set up between *Mallard's* cab and the dynamometer car. Edge then summoned the Westinghouse team members and explained to them for the first time the true nature of the trip. They were offered a taxi to Peterborough if they did not want to ride on the train as it attempted to retake the speed record on the way back. Every one of them refused and the train departed from Barkston South Junction at 4.15pm, when tea was served in the first-class section.

The footplate crew were dismayed to find speed limits in force at Grantham due to permanent way work, with a platelayer carrying out Sunday track maintenance, and the station was passed at just 18mph instead of the usual 60-70mph for express trains. However, fireman Bray made full use of the time to build a big fire.

It transpired that Gresley had been told about a "dead slow speed restriction at Grantham", but said the record attempt should still go ahead. Despite running at just 25mph at the beginning of the climb to Stoke Bank, the undaunted Duddington soon got *Mallard* up to 65mph with its boiler at full pressure. The engine accelerated up to Stoke summit and passed Stoke signalbox at 85mph.

The train then entered Stoke Tunnel and before the guard switched on the lights passengers were delighted by a firework display of red-hot cinders passing the windows after flying from *Mallard's* twin chimneys. The record keepers inside the dynamometer car saw that the A4 had passed Stoke summit at 6mph faster than *Silver Fox* when it had set its 113mph record at the same spot. *Mallard* then accelerated down Stoke Bank, faster than *Silver Fox* had done.

Within minutes, the speedometer reached 120mph, beating the LMS record. But Duddington and Bray knew they had to do more within the window of the next few minutes before the train had to slow down at the Essendine curves.

For one quarter of a mile, the needle in the dynamometer car recorded 126mph, at milepost 90¼ between Little Bytham and Essendine, 90 miles and 220 yards from King's Cross. The German record had now been broken as well, and permanently too.

It was reported that the train shook violently and crockery smashed to the floor. It was also claimed that windows were broken in Little Bytham station as *Mallard* powered through, spraying its platform with hot ashes. Edge was asked if the crew should try to go one better and hit 130mph, but with Essendine Tunnel approaching, he took the decision not to risk it. Through the intercom, the message was conveyed to Duddington to shut off. Essendine station was still passed at 108mph.

Minutes later, a distinctive smell conveyed the bad news of the day. The A4's middle big end bearing had run hot while developing 3000 cylinder hp, and it had to slow down as much as possible to reach Peterborough to avoid the locomotive being wrecked. There, it was found that the white metal had melted. Contrary to some accounts, the middle big end did not disintegrate, but merely overheated. The overheating may have been the result of the sudden shutting-off of steam at Essendine, leading to high-stress reversal on the pistons and driving rods.

An Ivatt Atlantic, No. 3290, took the train back to King's Cross. The national press had been tipped off about the achievement and was waiting on the platform. There, the footplate crew received a heroes' welcome, as news of their feat made headlines firstly throughout Britain and then around the world within hours of the train arriving back in London. Journalists seemed not to notice that they had arrived back on an Atlantic, not *Mallard*, and were taken into the dynamometer car where they were shown the physical proof of the speed record.

For days, the footplate crew were feted as celebrities, the equivalent of today's pop stars or millionaire footballers, but, modestly, both men considered the record run to be part of their everyday work, little more. Indeed, the day after their record run both were back at work on the footplate of another East Coast Main Line express. The press called *Mallard* the 'Blue Streak', a nickname which has stuck for the A4s.

Edge telephoned Gresley to convey the news. The records from the dynamometer were read and it was found that 126.1mph had been reached, but for just one second, over 60 yards. The LNER subsequently claimed only a peak average of 125mph. *Mallard* had also maintained 120mph over three miles, and an average of that speed over five, a magnificent feat in itself.

Writing in *The Railway Magazine* at the time, the railway author Cecil J Allen said: "The LNER, in its brilliant speed achievement of Sunday, July 3, carried its purpose into effect with such thoroughness as to leave the nearest British competitor some 11mph behind.

"The tremendous speed which was both attained and held for an average of 120mph for five miles is no mere fortuitous peak in the speed curve — it also provided a significant tribute to the efficiency of the Kylchap exhaust arrangements and double chimney with which *Mallard* is fitted.

"At 120 to 125mph, the driving wheels are revolving over 500 times a minute, and both to provide the steam for full regulator and 40% cut off at this speed as well as to get it out of the cylinders after use and up the chimney is a severe test of locomotive capacity.

"The speed record was a by-product, so to speak, of some important brake tests which required a succession of runs at high speed, and the stretch from Grantham to Peterborough was naturally chosen as the most suitable for the purpose."

Britain had invented the steam railway locomotive through Richard Trevithick in 1802, at Coalbrookdale in Shropshire, and 136 years later, the country's finest steam locomotive was proudly sitting on the top of the world. It was exactly what Britain needed. The Thirties were a decade dominated by the economic gloom of the Great Depression, which followed in the wake of the 1929 Wall Street Crash and led in other countries to the rise of authoritarian regimes with eventual catastrophic consequences. Gresley, *Mallard* and its crew proved that it was indeed possible to achieve again and come out on top of the world. What was more, the train proved that ordinary people like Duddington and Bray could 'have a go' and succeed big time.

Back in July 1938, the world, if only momentarily, seemed everyone's oyster again. *Mallard's* run was also the peak of the great glamorous expresses which highlighted what many see as the zenith of steam, symbolic of an era soon to be brought to a shuddering halt.

In Germany, both that country's newspapers and Nazi party officials were at first silent about *Mallard's* feat, but eventually worked out the excuse that *Mallard* had taken the world steam record only because it had been running downhill, whereas their country's locomotive had reached 124.5mph on the flat.

Yet no parameters had ever been set for speed records. *Mallard* was on record as being the fastest, and stayed that way.

The overheated bearing was quickly remetalled at New England shed in Peterborough, but as a precautionary measure the centre axle was also replaced at Doncaster. Nine days after the record run, *Mallard* returned to service.

The LNER and Gresley himself accepted the speed record as 125mph, but Cecil J Allen quoted the momentary speed of 126mph when writing in *The Railway Magazine* in March/April 1943. That speed is the one recorded on the plaque affixed to Mallard in 1948 in honour of its record achievement, and which it carries to this day.

There will forever be speculation as to what might have happened if that Sunday speed restriction had not been in place at Grantham. It was considered that had that been the case, 130mph could have been achieved, and that even before *Mallard's* run, such a speed would be possible with an A4.

Gresley wanted to try to set another new record the following year, but his ambition was scuppered by the build-up to and outbreak of the Second World War. Before *Mallard's* record run, it had been calculated that 130mph was indeed possible with an A4, but we will now never know for certain.

CHAPTER 8

Mallard after the milestone

MALLARD CONTINUED in service for another quarter of a century after its magical moment of world-beating glory. Like the other 34 A4s, it was fitted with streamlined valances when built. This side skirting was removed in the spring of 1942 to ease maintenance during the Second World War and on June 13 it was repainted into wartime black. The valances were restored in preservation.

The distinctive A4 chime whistles were removed from the class in 1942 and destroyed because the Government believed that they could become confused with air-raid sirens. No. 4468 was based at Doncaster until October 21, 1943, when it was reallocated to Grantham. Under the renumbering system of Gresley's successor Edward Thompson, it later became No. 22.

After Nationalisation in 1948, it was repainted into garter blue as British Railways No. E22 and on September 16, 1949, it became No. 60022. That year, the new national railway trialled the best locomotives from the 'Big Four' companies to find the best attributes of speed, power and efficiency with coal and water. One of the aims was to draw up new designs for the planned Standard series of locomotives, of which 999 were eventually built.

The express passenger locomotive designs to be compared were the LMS 'Princess Coronation' class, the A4s, the GWR 'Kings' and the Southern Railway's 'Merchant Navy' class. The three A4s that took part in the tests between April and June were *Mallard* No. 60022, now on its fourth boiler and third tender, and with a Flaman speed recorder refitted, No. 60033 *Seagull* and No. 60034 *Lord Faringdon*, all fitted with the Kylchap double blastpipe chimney arrangement.

On June 8, 1948, *Mallard* ran on the Waterloo-Exeter route. Despite being held back by a succession of red signals, its train was only 5½ minutes late and at Axminster it had reached 82mph. However, *Mallard* failed after the run and was replaced by *Seagull*. It also failed during a trial run on the Southern Region.

Mallard's final reallocation came on April 11, 1948, when it was moved to King's Cross. It was given a new corridor tender and headed non-stop expresses to Scotland.

In mid-1952, the garter blue livery was replaced with British Railways lined Brunswick green, a derivative of the GWR. *Mallard* hauled the last non-stop 'The Elizabethan' from King's Cross to Edinburgh Waverley on September 8, 1961. It completed the 392¾-mile journey nearly three minutes early, despite five permanent way slacks and two signal checks.

No. 60022's finest post-war moment came on September 19, 1961, when it produced one of the highest power outputs reached by a member of its class while taking the 2pm from King's Cross to Newcastle with 11 coaches. Climbing the 1-in-440 gradient from Tallington to Essendine on Stoke Bank, scene of its greatest triumph, it reached 78mph, and 82mph as the slopes eased beyond to Corby Glen. The estimated drawbar horse power (edhp) would have been around 2150, very high indeed for an A4, even those fitted with the Kylchap chimney.

It reached the 1-in-178 summit at 78mph, where 50-60mph was considered the norm. Thereby, it had achieved a record run up the legendary Stoke Bank, as opposed to down it. *Mallard* returned to the Waterloo-Exeter line for a Locomotive Club of Great Britain railtour on February 24, 1963. When finally withdrawn by British Railways from King's Cross shed on April 25 that year, it had covered 1,426,261 miles.

Mallard had been fitted with 12 boilers during its 25-year career. These boilers were Nos. 9024 (from construction), 8959 (from 4496 *Golden Shuttle*, June 13, 1942), 8907 (from 2511 *Silver King*, August 1, 1946), 8948 (from *Golden Plover*, March 5, 1948), 8957 (from 60009 *Union of South Africa*, September 16, 1949), 29282 (from 60028 *Walter K. Whigham*, January 10, 1951), 29301 (from 60019 *Bittern*, July 4, 1952), 29315 (from 60014 *Silver Link*, April 23, 1954), 29328 (new-build boiler, June 7, 1957), 29308 (from 60008 *Dwight D. Eisenhower*, August 27, 1958), 29310 (from 60009 *Union of South Africa*, March 9, 1960) and 27965 (again from 60009 *Union of South Africa*, August 10, 1961).

It had seven tenders, beginning with a non-corridor tender in 1938. It had corridor design tenders during its British Railways days and was fitted with a non-corridor tender in 1963 to recreate its original appearance. The tenders were: Nos. 5642 (March 3, 1938-March 14, 1939), 5639 (May 5, 1939-January 16, 1948), 5323 (March 5, 1948-March 12, 1953), 5648 (March 12, 1953-July 21, 1958), 5330 (August 27, 1958-May 30, 1962), 5651 (May 30, 1962-April 25 1963) and 5670 (current tender, masquerading as original tender 5642).

SAVED FOR THE NATION

With the demise of steam, the British Transport Commission was drawing up a list of locomotives to be preserved as part of a National Collection. When a particular locomotive type was identified for preservation, normally the first in the class would be saved. It was a foregone conclusion that an A4 Pacific would be preserved for posterity, but which one?

No. 60014 (2509) *Silver Link* was the first in the class and the second most famous... but *Mallard* held the record, and was therefore chosen, as an exception to the first-in-the-class rule. Both engines were among the first batch of King's Cross A4s to be withdrawn and neither was nominated for a new lease of life in Scotland, as was the case with other class members.

A4 withdrawals started in 1962 with the King's Cross engines, the terminus becoming a no-go area for steam from June 1963. *Mallard* quickly went into Doncaster Works for external restoration to original condition, complete with valances and garter blue livery as No. 4468, and ready to take pride of place in the new Museum of British Transport being planned at Clapham.

Billy Butlin was in the market for engines for display at his holiday camps, recognising the fact that despite its demise, steam still held a massive fascination for youngsters. He looked at some LMS Pacifics and then *Silver Link*. Withdrawn on December 29, 1962, the Eastern Region was unwilling to sell *Silver Link*, and quoted a price which was far too high, and it was subsequently scrapped. The term 'jobsworth' immediately comes to mind here.

Instead, Butlin dealt with the infinitely more co-operative London Midland Region and acquired two 'Duchesses', a 'Princess' and a 'Royal Scot', plus some Southern tank engines. *Mallard* entered Clapham Museum on February 29, 1964. That museum proved short lived, and was superseded by the National Railway Museum at York. *Mallard* made a return to the national network on April 12, 1975, when it was towed from London to York for static display.

In 1977, *Mallard* was displayed at York station to mark its centenary. During June 17-18, 1978, it visited Doncaster Works for an open day commemorating the 12th anniversary of 'The Plant'. With the half-centenary of its record run approaching, the NRM returned *Mallard* to working order in the Eighties.

The Friends of the National Railway Museum set up a Mallard 88 working party under the leadership of Andrew Roberts, and received backing from Scarborough Borough Council which was backing the launch of the 'Scarborough Spa Express' that year. The resort contributed around £35,000 towards the cost of the restoration of *Mallard*.

The restoration took place in a former diesel depot next to the museum which it had just acquired and a specialist contractor, Whitlam Insulation, was engaged to remove the asbestos lagging from the boiler. A pair of gearboxes for the Flaman speed recorder were obtained from the French Railway Museum at Mulhouse to replace the wooden mock-ups installed for museum display purposes.

Three contractors undertook the overhaul under the auspices of the museum's chief mechanical engineer John Bellwood but a decision had to be made about the extent of the restoration. In order to obtain an unconditional boiler certificate for main line running, many firebox stays would have had to have been replaced at great cost. However, one way around this was to restrict the locomotive to a limited number of operating days, cutting the cost.

RETURN TO STEAM

Marking the 10th anniversary of the NRM, *Mallard* moved under its own power, minus its boiler cladding, on September 27, 1985. On March 25, 1986, it returned to the main line, hauling a special train from York to Doncaster via Scarborough and Hull as a test run. Subsequently, it went to Doncaster Works for the weight distribution to be checked, returning to York in the night. It ran its first heritage era main line railtour on July 9, 1986, when it hauled British Rail's 'Scarborough Spa Express' from York to Scarborough and back via Hull and Goole.

On the outward journey, following a sprightly 69mph after Heslerton, it was brought to a stand at signals for more than 20 minutes at Weaverthorpe. Line speeds precluded any spirited running, but it still reached 74.5mph at Copmanthorpe. There were more York to Scarborough trips on August 31 and September 4, the latter returning with a cricket festival charter special. On October 4, 1986, *Mallard* ran from York to Marylebone via Sheffield, Derby, Birmingham and Banbury. There were three dining train trips, from Marylebone to Stratford-upon-Avon and back on October 12 and 26 and November 4.

On November 8, No. 4468 ran from Marylebone to York via Banbury, Birmingham, Derby and Sheffield. There were a handful of further runs in 1987. *Mallard* ran from York to Harrogate and Leeds on April 25, and hauled a Friends of the National Railway Museum 10th anniversary charter train the following day. May 16 saw *Mallard* hauling — appropriately in view of its designer's hobby — a Royal Society for the Protection of Birds special from York to Carnforth and back.

Mallard joined forces with BR Standard 9F 2-10-0 No. 92220 *Evening*

Star, the last main line steam locomotive built by British Railways, for a trip from York to Doncaster on October 2. The next day, both attended a Doncaster Works open day before returning to their York home.

The 50th anniversary celebrations for *Mallard* were staged in 1988. On May 9, it headed a Post Office special from Marylebone to Banbury, carrying a 'Postal Pullman' headboard. The train not only celebrated 150 years of sorting mail on the move but also the release of four stamps featuring transport in the 1930s, one, the 18p, depicting *Mallard*.

Coupled behind *Mallard* were Travelling Post Office sorting vehicles in their latest red livery. The special returned to Marylebone behind Class 47 No. 47515 *Night Mail*, while *Mallard* ran northwards to head another Post Office special, from Manchester to Scarborough, the following day. Meanwhile, preparations for celebrations to mark the 50th anniversary of *Mallard's* world speed record continued.

Several members of the original train crew from July 3, 1938 were tracked down and invited to join a special excursion from Doncaster to Scarborough on the exact 50th anniversary. British Rail chairman Sir Peter Parker agreed for a steam engine to take over from an electric locomotive on the East Coast Main Line north of Peterborough. However, because the new type of 25kV insulators used in the tunnels on the ECML during electrification were considered too heat sensitive, the changeover was instead arranged for Doncaster, from where *Mallard* would take the train on to Scarborough.

Hauling the train from King's Cross to Doncaster, and back from Doncaster again, was prototype Class 89 No. 89001, which was built at Crewe Works in 1986 and which has since been preserved by the AC Electric Group. Only one Class 89 was built. Echoing Gresley's birds theme, No. 89001 was officially named *Avocet* by Prime Minister Margaret Thatcher on January 16, 1989 at Sandy, Bedfordshire – the home of the Royal Society for the Protection of Birds (whose logo is an avocet). It was nicknamed 'Aardvark' although enthusiasts called it 'The Badger' because of its sloping front ends.

On board the special were driver Joe Duddington's granddaughter Jean Delaney and her son Matthew, and Tom Bray, the son of the fireman.

Thousands packed the lineside to glimpse *Mallard* pass by on the trip, which was undertaken at a modest 6omph. The driver for the trip was volunteer Derek Richardson. A massive birthday cake was prepared, and later given to Doncaster Royal Infirmary. *Mallard* steamed for the last time on August 27, 1988, and has since then remained a static exhibit.

The engine was taken out of the museum and displayed at an open weekend at Doncaster Works to mark its 150th anniversary on July 26-27, 2003. The weekend of July 5, 2008, saw *Mallard* brought outside the NRM for the first time in many years and displayed alongside the three other surviving A4s in Britain: *Bittern, Sir Nigel Gresley* and *Union of South Africa*, reuniting them all for the first time in the heritage era. The event marked the 70th anniversary of the speed record.

Mallard was displayed at the Locomotion museum in Shildon from late June 2010 until July 19, 2011, when it was returned to the Great Hall. A plan to allow it to visit the DB Museum in Nuremberg where it would have been displayed that summer alongside the surviving example of the German Class 0, whose world speed record it snatched away, failed to materialise.

FASTER THAN *MALLARD*?

Was *Mallard* really the fastest steam locomotive of all time? Railway speed records can be a notorious playing field that is anything but level. They tend to fall into the categories of official speed records, such as the 100mph set by *Flying Scotsman* in 1934, the unofficial, such as the 102.3mph claimed for *City of Truro* in 1904, and the semi-unofficial or rumoured.

Debate still rages as to whether the German record holder which reached 124.5mph on the level could have beaten *Mallard* on the same stretch of track, bearing in mind that No. 4468 recorded 126.1mph while going down Stoke Bank.

After the tragedy of the Preston rail crash of 1896 which brought to a swift end the Races to the North, railway companies perceived a public mood change in which the excitement about greater speeds gave way to fear. The GWR was reticent for several years to talk about the alleged record-breaking feat of *City of Truro* for this reason.

At first, Charles Rous-Marten kept quiet about the 102.3mph claim, and when he wrote an article that appeared in *The Railway Magazine* a month later, he merely described the trip as setting "the record of records". He wrote: "It is not desirable at present to publish the actual maximum rate that was reached on this memorable occasion," and restricted his account to reporting that the train reached the minimum of 62mph logged on the ascent of Whiteball summit.

Finally, the identity of the locomotive and the speed was revealed in the April 1908 edition of the magazine, but it was only in 1922 that the GWR finally publicly boasted about the feat of *City of Truro* and laid claim to the record. Yet even if Rous-Marten's timings were correct, was *City of Truro* really the first steam locomotive to break the 100mph barrier?

Five years earlier, a series of high-speed test runs on the Lancashire & Yorkshire Railway's Liverpool Exchange-Southport line used locomotives from John Aspinall's newly-introduced 'High Flyer' 4-4-2 class. It was reported that on July 15, 1899, one such train formed by No. 1392 and five coaches, and timed to leave Liverpool Exchange at 2.51pm, was recorded as passing milepost 17 in 12.75 mins.

While this gives a start-to-pass speed of 80mph, given the permanent 20mph restriction at Bank Hall and the 65mph restriction at Waterloo, it has been suggested that this train attained 100mph. The railway did not publish details or timings of this trip, which is recorded only through passing times unofficially noted by local enthusiasts. The late David Jenkinson, former head of education and research at the National Railway Museum, said: "It may well have been possible for an engine with driving wheels that size to achieve a feat like that on that particular route. You can probably place some credence on it."

There can be a huge gulf in credibility between official speed records and unofficial ones, the latter of which might be down to mere lineside gossip and speculation. On other occasions, it has been said that locomotive crews reached high speeds in defiance of speed restrictions, but played down the fact for fear of losing their jobs.

It was said that New York Central & Hudson River Railroad 4-4-0 No. 999 reached 112mph during an exhibition run of the 'Empire State Express' between Batavia and Buffalo on May 10, 1893, thereby becoming the world's first object on wheels to exceed 100mph. No. 999 was preserved in 1962, and is now displayed inside the main hall at the Chicago Museum of Science and Industry.

Pennsylvania Railroad E2 class 4-4-2 No. 7002 reached 127.1mph at Crestline in Ohio while hauling its 18-hour 'Pennsylvania Special' from New York City to Chicago on June 11, 1905, some have claimed. At the time, however, locomotives did not carry speedometers and speed was calculated by measuring time between mile markers, so the claim could not be officially substantiated. The *New York Times* reported on June 14, 1905 that the claims published in the Chicago press had been exaggerated, and the real speed was closer to 70-80mph.

On July 20, 1934, Chicago, Milwaukee, St Paul and Pacific Railroad 4-6-4 No. 6402 hauled a regular 380-ton service train from Chicago to Milwaukee, hauling the train over the 85 miles in 67 minutes and 37 seconds, reaching a maximum speed of 103mph as a test to see if it were possible. British author Bryan Benn believes it is the first claim of more than 100mph (in which the surviving documentation strongly indicates its accuracy). If true, it beat *Flying Scotsman's* feat on Stoke Bank by a few months.

The success of this test run led to the Chicago, Milwaukee, St Paul and Pacific Railroad launching its 'Hiawatha' express in 1935, using four streamlined Alco 4-4-2s specially built for the job. Indeed, they were the world's first locomotives purpose-built for daily operation at more than 100mph, with a 6½-hour run between Minneapolis and Chicago, and designed for 120mph. In its day, 'Hiawatha' was the fastest scheduled express train in the world.

A recorded run with a dynamometer car behind locomotive No. 2 on May 15, 1935, from Milwaukee and Wisconsin saw 112.5mph recorded over a 14-mile stretch, making it the first steam locomotive to officially exceed 110mph.

They were followed in service by the six F7 streamlined 4-6-4s which were introduced in 1939 and ran at speeds in excess of 100mph on a daily basis. One was recorded at 125mph on a run between Chicago and Milwaukee after managing an average of 120mph for 4½ miles, a whisker short of *Mallard's* record. The Pennsylvania Railroad's streamlined art deco S1 6-4-4-6 prototype was unofficially clocked at 127.1mph. An article which appeared in the December 1941 issue of *Popular Mechanics* magazine claimed it reached 133.4mph and there are tales that it may have even topped 140mph, but none of these claims was supported by any documentary proof and they were not believed by experts. Another story has it that S1 exceeded 156mph on the Fort Wayne-Chicago Railroad, leading to the company being fined, but again, no records survive.

How many other so-called 'instances' have passed into the oblivion of history we shall never know. There is an unconfirmed story that on arrival at King's Cross with a late-running Up express, the driver and fireman of A4 No. 60017 *Silver Fox* were immediately suspended for two weeks for having been clocked at 130mph on Stoke Bank. Intriguingly, issue 732 of *The Journal of the Stephenson Locomotive Society*, published in July/August 1988, records a statement made by a member of "impeccable integrity". It was said that accomplished driver Bill Hoole, during his last week of British Railways service, took an A4 down Stoke Bank at 132mph.

The Eastern Region would not confirm or deny that such a speed had been reached. Sceptics point to the slight curve and track fittings at Essendine which would have precluded such a feat, but from where did the story emanate? It is easy and logical to dismiss lineside gossip as rumour and wild speculation but in most cases, as a railway magazine editor, this author has virtually always found it to be much nearer the mark than you might expect.

CHAPTER NINE

The fortunate five

THIRTY-FIVE GRESLEY A4 streamlined Pacifics were built in total. One of them, No. 4469 *Sir Ralph Wedgwood*, outshopped on August 30, 1938, at Gadwall and renamed in March 1939, was destroyed in a Luftwaffe raid on York on June 6, 1942.

That left 34 to fly the flag on the East Coast Main Line into the early Sixties, when they were ousted by diesel traction in the form of the Class 55 Deltics. The first five withdrawals, in December 1963, were No. 60014 *Silver Link*, No. 60028 *Walter K. Whigham*, No. 60003 *Andrew K. McCosh*, No. 60030 *Golden Fleece* and No. 60033 *Seagull*. The rest of the class was withdrawn between 1963 and 1966. The last six in service were No. 60004 *William Whitelaw*, No. 60007 *Sir Nigel Gresley*, No. 60009 *Union of South Africa*, No. 60019 *Bittern*, No. 60024 *Kingfisher* and No. 60034 *Lord Faringdon*. No. 60019 and 60024 were the last to be withdrawn, in September 1966.

As we know, six survived into preservation. Plans to save *Mallard* for the National Collection had been made as early as 1960 but, as we saw, there was no second life for the legendary class doyen, No. 2509 *Silver Link*.

Had three of the A4s not been bought by British enthusiasts and two obtained by museums in north America, *Mallard* would be the sole representative of one of the most magnificent locomotive classes of any description. To those who saved each of the 'fortunate five' we owe an immense debt of gratitude.

On July 3, 2013, the exact anniversary of *Mallard's* test run, thanks to the efforts of former director Steve Davies and his team at the National Railway Museum, plus a host of other companies involved in the project to temporarily repatriate *Dwight D. Eisenhower* and *Dominion of Canada* from North America, all six surviving A4s were reunited in the museum at York.

It was one of the most spectacular and poignant moments in the history of railway preservation. Nearly three years of planning had finally come to fruition in honour of Britain's record holder. The story of *Mallard* can never be anything but legendary. However, the other five who joined No. 4468 around the turntable in the Great Hall also have their tales to tell.

SIR NIGEL GRESLEY

Writer K Risdon Prentice, co-author of Locomotives of the LNER 1923-37, which was published by the Railway Correspondence & Travel Society, came up with the idea of naming the 100th Gresley Pacific after the great man himself. Without him, No. 4498 would probably have been named *Bittern*. To have an engine named after him was one of the greatest honours that could be bestowed on a locomotive engineer. And who can argue that this honour was not richly deserved?

It was posted to King's Cross shed on November 30, 1937, although the move was not made permanent until February 25, 1938. From 'Top Shed', No. 4498 worked express passenger duties including the 'Silver Jubilee', 'Coronation' and 'Flying Scotsman' and it quickly gained a reputation for speed and power. As with the earlier A4s, No. 4498 was built with single chimney and side valances covering the wheels. The valances were removed as an austerity era aid to maintenance on February 21, 1942.

Like the other A4s, *Sir Nigel Gresley* carried many liveries throughout its career. First appearing in the standard LNER garter blue of the A4 Pacifics with silver gilt letters, new numbers and letters for the tender in stainless steel were added in a general overhaul on January 16, 1939.

The locomotive was repainted into wartime black with LNER markings on February 21, 1942. The next repaint was into black with NE markings on October 20, 1943, as a cutback. After the war, the LNER garter blue livery with red and white lining was reapplied on March 6, 1947. After Nationalisation, *Sir Nigel Gresley* was painted into British Railways dark blue with black and white lining on September 27, 1950. The final livery change saw it repainted into British Railways Brunswick green livery on April 17, 1952.

Sir Nigel Gresley was used for the opening of the Rugby testing station between August and October 1948. It was also reallocated to Grantham between April 1944 and June 1950.

By then renumbered 60007, it was placed onto the rollers without its tender and run up to high speeds to monitor the coal and water usage.

It has been said that driver Bill Hoole took No. 60007 down Stoke Bank at a speed of 117mph with the 'Tees-Tyne Pullman', well above the 90mph limit, in November 1955. A civil engineer with a Hallade Track recording instrument was on board the train, but the device was not designed for recording such speeds. Disciplinary action against the footplate crew was avoided only because its accuracy was questioned.

No. 60007 received a double chimney and Kylchap double blastpipe on December 13, 1957. Its finest moment, however, was yet to come. When it came less than two years later, it did both *Mallard* and the legacy of its designer proud. *Mallard's* record was never broken, as the urge to set new steam records vanished with the Second World War.

Gresley himself understandably suffered from overwork towards the end of the Thirties. While he found time to visit Paris to discuss locomotive design with French engineers, and South Africa to see the Metropolitan-Vickers electric locomotives in action there, he did not take time off for the shooting holidays he so much enjoyed.

He developed chronic bronchitis and began to have difficulty in walking, while his heart began to fail. He took a last holiday in Devon with his daughter Vi, and managed to see his last two steam locomotives unveiled on February 19, 1941. One of them was the first of only two V4 class 2-6-2s built for mixed traffic use.

It was Gresley's last design for the LNER. Similar to the hugely successful V2 2-6-2s, the V4 was a lightweight version with greater route availability which could go anywhere over the LNER network. The first engine, No. 3401 *Bantam Cock*, had a scaled-down version of the Gresley Pacific boiler. The second, No. 3402, was unofficially named *Bantam Hen*. The type was tried on the Great Eastern section of the LNER and was considered to be superior to the B17 4-6-0s.

The second was Gresley's first venture into electric traction, in the form of Bo-Bo No. 6701, which was powered for the 1500V DC overhead system proposed for the conversion of the Woodhead route from Manchester to Sheffield. Not completed until 1954, this locomotive, the forerunner of the EM1 class, was loaned to the Dutch State Railways to help with its postwar shortage of locomotives from 1945-54 and named *Tommy*. Returning home to take its place on the Woodhead route fleet, it was renumbered 26000 by British Railways.

Had fate taken a different turn, would Gresley have switched his emphasis towards electric and maybe diesel traction after developing his A4 Pacifics to show that steam could do the same job as the German high-speed railcars, if not better? Might he have called for all-out electrification of the East Coast Main Line?

Gresley died after a short illness at his then home at Watton-at-Stone on April 5, 1941, in the presence of his son Roger. He was buried by the side of his wife Ethel in his home village of Netherseal, Derbyshire, in the village cemetery beneath the Boscobel Oak. This tree is descended from the famous oak tree at Boscobel House in Shropshire, in which Charles II hid after fleeing from the scene of his defeat at the Battle of Worcester in 1651.

Nigel was the last Gresley to be buried there. The same day, his business colleagues and friends attended a memorial service at Chelsea Old Church in London. A week later, the church was badly damaged during the blitz.

THE POST-WAR STEAM RECORD

Sadly, Gresley never realised his ambition to set a new 130mph record with an A4. Neither did his successor Edward Thompson proceed with building any more of his V2s, instead opting for his own B1 4-6-0 design. Both V4s were scrapped in 1957 when their boilers became due for renewal, although The A1 Steam Locomotive Trust, 21st-century builder and operator of new Peppercorn A1 Pacific No. 60163 *Tornado*, aims to build a third V4 to fill another major gap in the heritage steam fleet.

The A4 named in honour of Gresley set a new post-war steam record on where else but Stoke Bank. With the emergence of diesels on the East Coast Main Line taking over express passenger duties, it was decided to hold a farewell trip for steam. This was arranged to coincide with the golden jubilee of the Stephenson Locomotive Society.

Sir Nigel Gresley was chosen to haul the tour and was sent to Doncaster Works to be overhauled for the purpose. Bill Hoole, No. 60007's normal driver, was rostered to drive it. Earlier, on June 3, 1958, he had driven *Sir Nigel Gresley* as it hauled the Royal Train from King's Cross to York overnight with the Queen on board.

Hoole had begun his career on the Cheshire Lines Committee as an engine cleaner and worked his way up to become a top link driver at King's Cross. For the farewell special, the British Railways civil engineer agreed for the speed limits to be relaxed over certain sections of the route, and a maximum of 110mph was to be allowed down Stoke Bank.

The eight-coach train departed King's Cross on Saturday, May 23, 1959, with Hoole assisted by fireman Alf Hancox. It was claimed that it reached 100mph after Stevenage on the outward journey to Doncaster, and ascending Stoke Bank it hit 83mph between Essendine and Little Bytham. On the return leg, Stoke summit was passed at 75mph, with the speedometer rising to 99mph before Corby Glen, reaching 109mph by Little Bytham. It seemed that it was going for the record. However, those in control of the train were concerned about the safety of the 400 passengers on board and would not allow Hoole to go beyond the officially sanctioned limit of the day.

When the train reached 112mph, Alan Pegler, a member of the Eastern Region board who was on the footplate, signalled to Inspector Bert Dixon that Hoole must ease off. The 12.3 miles from Corby Glen to Tallington were covered in just seven minutes six seconds at an average of 104mph, arguably the fastest ever time between those points by a steam locomotive, beating even *Mallard* in this respect. Beyond Tempsford, 100mph was reached for the third time on the tour. The train arrived back at

King's Cross four minutes early having taken 137 minutes 38 seconds from Doncaster, averaging 68mph over the 156 miles. This time round there was no *Mallard*-style hot big end problem and No. 60007 was fit to return to traffic the next day. The new official post-war steam record of 112mph remains to this day.

Businessman Alan Pegler had begun to run railway enthusiast excursions from 1951 and his success in this field led him to be appointed to the British Transport Commission's Eastern area board four years later, hence his place on the footplate that day. Pegler is better known not only as the man who saved the Ffestiniog Railway in the early Fifties, but also as the man who, in 1963, bought Gresley A3 Pacific No. 4472 *Flying Scotsman* from British Railways.

Hoole knew another Ffestiniog preservation pioneer, Allan Garraway. After Hoole returned from British Railways in 1959, he started a new career in retirement as a driver for the Ffestiniog. He died in 1979 and is buried in Minffordd cemetery, his gravestone stating 'Bill Hoole: Engineman Extraordinary'.

A Smith-Stone type speed recorder was fitted to No. 60007 on June 30, 1960. After King's Cross shed closed, No. 60007 moved to New England shed at Peterborough on June 16, 1963. On July 6 that year, No. 60007 hit 103mph when running down Stoke Bank with the Locomotive Club of Great Britain's Mallard Commemorative Railtour from King's Cross to London and back. Another move saw it transferred on October 20, 1963, to St Margarets shed, from which it hauled Edinburgh-Aberdeen trains. Its final allocation was Aberdeen from July 20, 1964.

SAVED FROM SCRAPPING

Sir Nigel Gresley was withdrawn from British Railways service on February 1, 1966. A group of enthusiasts began efforts to save it under the banner of the A4 Preservation Society, which first met in October 1964 to prevent it from being scrapped. The idea was to emulate Pegler's feat in buying *Flying Scotsman* and using it for enthusiast specials.

On October 23, 1965, the society ran a railtour from Manchester to Paddington and specially asked for No. 60007 to haul it. *Sir Nigel Gresley's* last-known duty for British Railways in revenue-earning service was the 5.30pm Aberdeen to Perth run on January 7, 1966. When it was withdrawn, it had run around 1.5 million miles in traffic. It was condemned on February 1 that year.

After the group bought the locomotive on March 1966, it was moved to Crewe Works for overhaul, hauled there by an LMS 'Black Five' 4-6-0, and while at Crewe it was given the six driving wheels from sister A4 No. 60026 *Miles Beevor* because they were in far better condition. Also in the works being cosmetically restored was No. 60010 *Dominion of Canada*.

Sir Nigel Gresley undertook trial runs in the first complete week in March 1967, and later that month worked the late-night Crewe to Preston parcels train. Once it was back in traffic, the society turned itself into the A4 Locomotive Society Limited. Later that year it ran a series of railtours around the country, including trips to Weymouth and Aberdeen, and made a comeback to the East Coast Main Line on July 23, 1967.

After Carnforth's steam shed closed, it became a popular heritage railway museum called Steamtown. From there, once British Rail had relaxed its 1968 steam ban, *Sir Nigel Gresley* ran main line railtours once again. In April 1972, No. 4498 was reunited with Hoole at Carnforth, and he drove it up and down the half-mile Steamtown running line. In August 1975, No. 4498 took part in the Rail 150 Cavalcade at Shildon.

When the Post Office launched its Famous Trains stamps, *Sir Nigel Gresley* was not only depicted on one of them but was also chosen to haul a series of special trains between Marylebone and Stratford-upon-Avon in late January 1985. No. 4498 and *Flying Scotsman* were briefly joined on shed at Marylebone by no less than *Mallard* on October 11, 1986. During the Nineties, No. 60007 became the only A4 to be fitted with steam heating on the front, enabling tender-first running on heritage railways which do not have turning facilities.

No. 60007 became the first steam locomotive of the preservation era to have worked up Shap summit on the West Coast Main Line in 1995 and four years later it hauled a special train to mark the 40th anniversary of its record run down Stoke Bank. Two years after that, in 2001, it was withdrawn from traffic for overhaul — a process which cost £810,000 and which was completed in 2006. On June 18, 2012, it carried the Olympic torch over the NYMR.

At the time of writing, No. 60007 was owned by the Sir Nigel Gresley Locomotive Preservation Trust Ltd and operated by the A4 Locomotive Society Ltd. It was withdrawn from service in September 2015 when its boiler ticket expired, and was moved to the works at the National Railway Museum in York for its 10-year overhaul to be carried out – due for completion in 2022. For the record, *Sir Nigel Gresley* has had 12 boilers, No. 27966 from No. 60016 *Silver King* being the last to be fitted on October 25, 1962; and two tenders, No. 5329 from new and No. 5324 from August 1943.

BITTERN

Built at Doncaster Works as works number 1866 and outshopped on December 18, 1937, in standard garter blue livery, *Bittern* was originally numbered 4464. Like most other A4s, it was fitted with side valances and a single chimney from new. Repainted into wartime black on November 14, 1941, after its valances had been removed, its tender was modified on May 22, 1943, leaving it with the basic markings NE.

In the past, it has been claimed that this austerity measure was done to confuse wartime spies, but most observers believe it was simply to save scarce materials and labour by reducing the number of letters by half. *Bittern* was renumbered 19 on August 16, 1946, under Edward Thompson's 1946 renumbering scheme and after Nationalisation in 1948 British Railways added 60000 to its number on October 10 that year.

The locomotive was repainted into LNER postwar garter blue with extra red and white lining on March 7, 1947, and its next livery change came on July 28, 1950, when it was repainted into British Railways dark blue with black and white lining. Its last livery change in the steam era was on February 12, 1952, when it was painted Brunswick green, in which it hauled the 'Talisman'. First allocated to Heaton shed, from where it was used on the 'Flying Scotsman' train, it moved to Gateshead in March 1943, St Margarets on October 28, 1963, and Aberdeen Ferryhill on November 10, 1963.

Bittern was equipped with a double chimney with a Kylchap double blastpipe on September 6, 1957, Automatic Warning System apparatus on December 13, 1958, and a speed indicator on September 6, 1960. It had 14 boilers during its career. The second to be fitted was No. 9025 from No. 4469 *Sir Ralph Wedgwood* after it had been destroyed at York depot during the Luftwaffe raid on June 6, 1942. On November 30, 1954, it was fitted with boiler No. 29279 from No. 60009 *Union of South Africa*, and on September 6, 1957, with boiler No. 29315 from none other than *Mallard*. However, it always had the same tender, the non-corridor No. 5638.

From Ferryhill, *Bittern* was used on the Aberdeen to Glasgow and Edinburgh services, which ended in 1966. It headed the last A4 Glasgow to Aberdeen and back service on September 3, 1966, when it was withdrawn. Scottish A4 No. 60024 *Kingfisher* worked the Aberdeen to Edinburgh leg of a two-day railtour from London next day. On arrival at Edinburgh, *Bittern* took over the train and headed for York, where it entered into the ownership of Geoffrey Drury.

Kingfisher, sadly, was scrapped, but *Bittern* became the first preserved A4 to haul a main line railtour, as it was used on tours out of York in 1966/67. However, when bought, it had badly cracked frames and its Indian summer back on the main line soon came to an end. The problem with the frames was known to BR, but only light repairs were made since with the end of steam it would have been uneconomic to completely repair the locomotive. Accordingly, its career in preservation has been hampered until recent years when the important repairs had been done to bring it back up to main line standard.

After buying *Bittern*, Geoff Drury then switched his attention to Peppercorn A2 No. 60532 *Blue Peter* and bought it from British Rail in 1968. Both found a new home at the now closed Dinting Railway Centre near Glossop in Derbyshire and were looked after by the North Eastern Locomotive Preservation Group. While *Blue Peter* found its way back onto the national network, *Bittern* was cosmetically restored as the far more famous No. 2509 *Silver Link*.

In 1995, *Bittern* was moved to the Great Central Railway at Loughborough to be restored to working order, but reached only a partial stage of dismantling. Eventually, the locomotive was bought as a kit of parts by the late pharmaceuticals entrepreneur Dr Tony Marchington, one-time owner and restorer of *Flying Scotsman*. After the overhaul of No. 4472 overran its budget to the £1 million mark, Marchington sold *Bittern* on to multi-millionaire enthusiast Jeremy Hosking in January 2001.

Hosking moved it to Ropley Works on the Mid-Hants Railway and this was where serious restoration work began. *Bittern* steamed for the first time since the Seventies on May 19, 2007, outshopped in British Railways Brunswick green and at first hauling services on the Mid-Hants. After successfully completing main line test runs, *Bittern* made its revenue-earning comeback on the national network on December 1, 2007, on a charter from King's Cross to York.

During the major overhaul which returned the engine to traffic in 2007, the tender was rebuilt as a corridor version to allow extra flexibility of operations. A second tender was coupled to *Bittern* on July 25, 2009, allowing it to run all 188 miles from London to York non-stop. With the first tender having a water capacity of 5000 gallons and coal, and the second tender only used for carrying an extra 9000 gallons of water, it was thought that this would give *Bittern* a range of about 250 miles.

On the trip, the engine carried a 'Brighton Belle' headboard to draw attention to the 5BEL Trust's ground-breaking restoration of a five-car 'Brighton Belle' EMU set, Britain's only electric Pullman train, which is supported by Jeremy Hosking. *Heritage Railway* magazine exclusively revealed in 2011 that Jeremy Hosking had ordered *Bittern* to receive another identity exchange, becoming No. 4492 *Dominion of New Zealand*, with its *Silver Link* identity valances refitted and the repainting of the locomotive into LNER garter blue with the wheels in their original red colouring and steel lettering and numbers on the sides. As the original 4492 had a New Zealand Government Railways five-chime whistle fitted shortly after its introduction to service in 1937, a suitable whistle was borrowed from the Glenbrook Vintage Railway in New Zealand.

Dominion of New Zealand had, like *Union of South Africa*, been one of five A4s named after Commonwealth countries to pull the 'Coronation', which marked the accession of George VI in 1937. It reverted back to its identity of No. 4464 *Bittern* in spring 2012, but kept its garter blue livery. In late spring and early summer 2013, *Bittern* became the first officially sanctioned 90mph steam locomotive of the post-1971 era. At the time of writing, *Bittern's* ticket had expired, and it was in storage at Jeremy Hosking's new One:One Collection museum which has been developed in the iconic former Hornby models building in Margate's Westwood retail park.

UNION OF SOUTH AFRICA

No. 4488 *Union of South Africa* entered service on June 29, 1937, the first of five engines nominated for service on the 'Coronation' King's Cross-Edinburgh service, carrying garter blue livery with red wheels and stainless steel lettering, numerals and trim, and bearing a 'Commonwealth' name. Continuing the bird theme, the locomotive had previously been allocated the name *Osprey* on April 17, 1937, but by the time it was outshopped, it had been renamed.

The works number of *Union of South Africa* was 1853; the plaques are located in the cab itself and not on the exterior cabsides as is the usual practice. The next livery applied was LNER wartime black on March 21, 1942, and altered on August 14, 1943, when the tender letters became NE. The garter blue livery with red and white lining was reapplied on February 21, 1947.

The locomotive was renumbered 9 on January 12, 1946, and is still referred to colloquially on the lineside as 'Number 9'. It gained a stainless steel number 9 at this stage. British Railways express passenger blue livery was applied on August 4, 1949, and Brunswick green livery on October 2, 1952. It has worn this livery ever since.

The springbok plaque on the side of the locomotive was donated on April 12, 1954, by a Bloemfontein newspaper proprietor. Only the one plaque was fitted on the left-hand side of the locomotive. The position has changed on a couple of occasions; it was originally on the boiler side, being moved to the cabsides in preservation.

Recently, the plaque has reverted to the historically correct position. *Union of South Africa* was first allocated to Haymarket shed, remaining there until being transferred to Aberdeen Ferryhill in May 1962. No. 60009 had a double chimney fitted on November 18, 1958, 20 years after *Mallard* was similarly equipped. As safety requirements were tightened after the

One of the world's first Pacific locomotives, an example of the New Zealand Railways Department's Q class supplied by the Baldwin Locomotive Works of Philadelphia in 1901.

GWR No. 111 *The Great Bear*, Britain's first Pacific. GREAT WESTERN TRUST

The US classic that inspired Nigel Gresley: a Pennsylvania Railroad K4s-hauled train pauses at Aberdeen, Maryland on April 26, 1944.

The exterior of King's Cross station as seen during 1870-1900. ENGLISH HERITAGE

A Great Northern Stirling 4-2-2, of which 53 were built at Doncaster between 1870 and 1895. Patrick Stirling's singles – the trademark of which was the huge single driving wheel – brought the Great Northern Railway a huge reputation for speed in their day. A HISGETT COLLECTION

Nigel Gresley pictured during a family picnic accompanied by his grandson Tim Godfrey and the family dog. TIM GODFREY COLLECTION

Netherseal rectory, where Nigel Gresley spent his childhood, and a blue plaque recording the fact. ROBIN JONES

DERBYSHIRE COUNTY COUNCIL

SIR NIGEL GRESLEY
1876 - 1941

Pioneering railway engineer

Designed the Mallard and Flying
Scotsman steam locomotives
Advanced the modernisation of
Britain's railway network

Spent his childhood
at this rectory

The first Gresley Pacific was No. 1470 (LNER 4470) *Great Northern*, seen leaving Wood Green tunnel on a Down express in 1930. NRM

Greeting the triumphant footplate crew of No. 4472 *Flying Scotsman*, driver W Sparshatt and fireman R Webster, back at King's Cross after it hit 100mph on November 30, 1934. It was a decade in which ordinary locomotive crews acquired celebrity status overnight, the equivalent of today's rock stars or footballers. NRM

A1 No. 4472 *Flying Scotsman* ready for display at the British Empire Exhibition at Wembley in 1924.

One of several classic posters produced by the LNER to promote its ground-breaking London to Edinburgh services. NRM

The wedge-shaped streamlined petrol railcar that inspired the world's fastest steam locomotive: a Bugatti railcar depicted in action in the 1930s.

Racing car designer Ettore Bugatti.

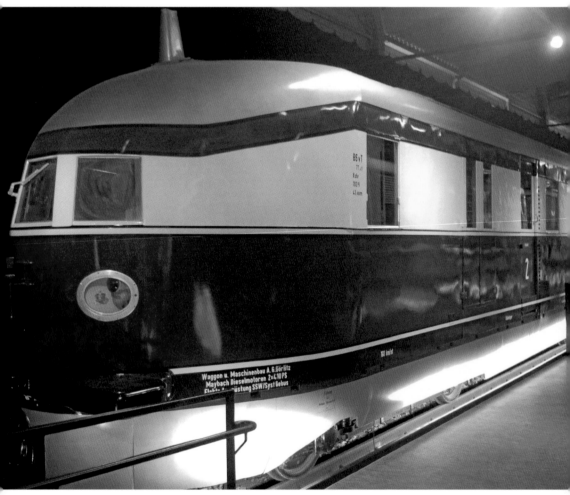

Germany's legendary 'Flying Hamburger': only the driver's cab, the engine compartment and the saloon of one vehicle are preserved, at the DB Museum in Nuremberg. ROBIN JONES

The first of Nigel Gresley's A4s: No. 2509 *Silver Link*, pictured at Grantham in July 1937. J WHALEY/COLOUR-RAIL

A4 Pacific No. 2509 *Silver Link* entered service on September 7, 1935, in silver grey livery, and on September 27, worked the inaugural Down 'Silver Jubilee', commemorating King George V's silver jubilee. The train was booked to run from King's Cross to Newcastle in four hours at an average speed of 67.08mph, and the inaugural press run averaged 100mph for 43 miles and touched 112mph. FE BOX/NRM

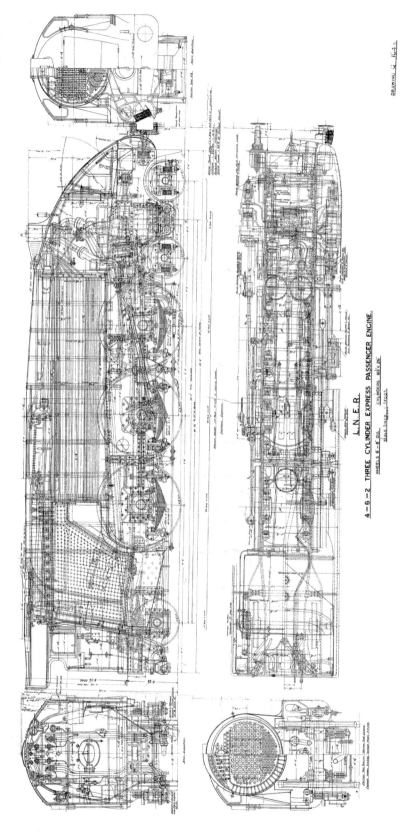

CLASS A — 4

DRAWING 2

L.N.E.R.
4—6—2 THREE CYLINDER EXPRESS PASSENGER ENGINE.
WHEELS 6'-8" DIA.   CYLINDERS 18½"x 26"
SCALE ⅛in = 1 foot

The drawings for the new A4 streamlined Pacifics. NRM

The inaugural run of the 'Silver Jubilee' express on September 27, 1935, with Sir Nigel Gresley standing on the footplate of A4 No. 2509 *Silver Link*. NRM

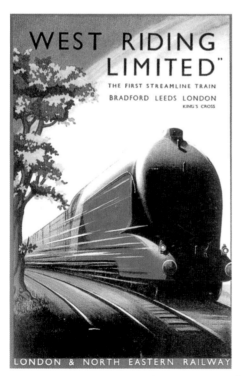

A classic LNER poster advertising the 'West Riding Limited' which started on September 27, 1937 when the first train was hauled by A4 No. 4492 *Dominion of New Zealand* which had entered service only three months earlier. NRM

William Stanier, chief mechanical engineer of the LMS, who designed the streamlined Princess Coronation Pacifics as an answer to Gresley's A4s. Like Gresley, he was also knighted, on February 9, 1943, and also had one of his own engines named after him. No. 6256, the penultimate streamlined Princess Coronation, became *Sir William Stanier FRS (Fellow of the Royal Society)*.

LMS Princess Coronation Pacific No. 6220 leaves
London with the June 29, 1937, test train which took
a curve at Crewe so fast in defiance of the speed
restriction that the dining car crockery was smashed.

The great rivals meet: re-streamlined LMS Princess Coronation Pacific No. 6229 *Duchess of Hamilton*, which once masqueraded as No. 6220 on a tour of North America, alongside A4 No. 4468 *Mallard* inside the Great Hall at the National Railway Museum in 2009. BRIAN SHARPE

LMS Princess Royal Pacific No. 46201 *Princess Elizabeth* passes Harthorpe near Beattock with the Down 'Royal Scot' in 1960. ERIC TREACY/NRM

Right: Passengers having their tickets checked before boarding the 'Coronation Scot.' LMS

Below: Proud workers and staff at the Borsig locomotive factory in Berlin-Tegel line up alongside newly-outshopped streamlined Class 05 4-6-4 No. 05001.

Above: In 1935, No. 05001 was presented at the One Hundred Years of German Railways propaganda exhibition in Nuremberg. The sole surviving member of the class, it is now a static exhibit inside the Deutsche Bahn Museum in the city. ROBIN JONES

Right: The front of the streamlined No. 05001. ROBIN JONES

Right: Faces of evil: Heinrich Himmler and Reinhard Heydrich, who masterminded the Holocaust with railways as a primary tool, and were both aboard the VIP trip on which Class 05 4-6-4 No. 050002 set a new world speed record on May 11, 1936.

Mallard about to set off from Barkston Junction South on its attempt to regain both the British and world steam speed records on July 3, 1938. NRM

TELEPHONE TERMINUS 4200
Ext: 3600
TELEGRAPHIC ADDRESS
"MECHANICAL, C/o NORTHEASTERN RAIL, LONDON"

REFERENCE
2/1/135.XII

THE CHIEF MECHANICAL ENGINEER

LONDON & NORTH EASTERN RAILWAY

KING'S CROSS STATION

LONDON N. 1

28th June, 1938.

The Mechanical Engineer,
DARLINGTON.

WESTINGHOUSE QUICK SERVICE APPLICATION VALVES.

    With reference to telephone conversation with your office: I am proposing to carry out brake tests with No.103 High Speed Set and Engine No.4468 on Sunday next between London and Peterboro', making stops at the points shown below, and I should be glad if you would arrange for the Dynamometer Car run with the train and take the necessary observations :-

Down		Up	
Welwyn Garden City	78 m.p.h.	Connington	60 m.p.h.
Stevenage	69 "	Tempsford	83 "
Langford Bridge	89 "	Wymondley	74 "
Holme	93 "	Digswell	74 "

    The train will be fitted with Westinghouse Quick Service Application Valves to the brake cylinders, allowing air to be admitted direct to each cylinder, and it is desirable that the Dynamometer Car should be similarly equipped. Suitable valves will be provided by the Westinghouse Company, and I should be glad if you would arrange for the car to be sent up to London as early as possible for the valves to be fitted.

    In previous tests with these quick service valves, it has been found necessary to remove the small diameter choke from the van valves, as the inrush of air direct to the cylinders, combined with the entry of air down the train pipe, causes premature operation of the van valves and renders proper control of the brake rather difficult. It will therefore be necessary for the choke to be removed from the van valve in the Dynamometer car for these tests, and I should be glad if you would arrange for this to be done.

    Whilst the brake trials will be made south of Peterborough, it is proposed to run the train to Barkeston and back in order that a fast run down the bank from Stoke tunnel to Peterborough may be recorded.

    I should be glad if you would make the necessary arrangements so far as you are concerned.

The historic letter of June 28, 1938, requesting the use of No. 4468 *Mallard* on a test run five days later. No mention is made of an attempt at the world speed record.

Mallard reaching 126mph on Stoke Bank as captured by one of Gresley's lineside team on July 3, 1938. NRM

To celebrate the 75th anniversary of *Mallard's* world steam record run, the National Railway Museum issued a print of a watercolour painting of the event by Australian railway artist, illustrator, amateur cinematographer and steam enthusiast Phil Belbin (1925-1993).

Little Bytham station, where it was said that windows were shattered as *Mallard* roared through on its record run.

The NER dynamometer car which recorded *Mallard's* record is displayed inside the Great Hall at the National Railway Museum. Equipment in the vehicle calculated speed by measuring the distance covered in a given period of time. The measurements were made continually and automatically on a roll of paper from which the results could be analysed afterwards. ROBIN JONES

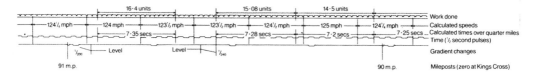

	16·4 units		15·08 units		14·5 units		Work done
124¼ mph	124 mph	123½ mph	123½ mph	124½ mph	125 mph	124¼ mph	Calculated speeds
	7·35 secs		7·28 secs		7·2 secs	7·25 secs	Calculated times over quarter miles
							Time (½ second pulses)
	Level	Level					Gradient changes
91 m.p.	¹⁄₂₀₀	¹⁄₂₄₀			90 m.p.		Mileposts (zero at Kings Cross)

Part of the dynamometer car recording roll from *Mallard's* record run on July 3, 1938. The distance was determined by the movement of the paper beneath the recording pens, which was done mechanically by gears driven directly by the vehicle's ninth wheel. On high-speed runs, the gearing was selected to allow the paper to move at 2ft for every mile travelled. A secondary distance recording involved an observer pressing a button at the end of an electric lead as each landmark, such as mileposts, was passed, in order to align the chart with the gradient profile of the distance covered. NRM

The victorious *Mallard* crew from left to right: driver Joe Duddington, fireman Tommy Bray, inspector Sam Jenkins, the train guard and other members of the team at Peterborough after setting a new world record on July 3, 1938. NRM

The plaque fixed to *Mallard* in 1948 in honour of its world steam speed record, which it states is 126mph. ROBIN JONES

In the Nineties, this sign was erected on Stoke Bank to mark the spot where *Mallard* set a new world steam speed record. ROBIN JONES

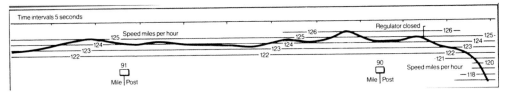

Time intervals 5 seconds

Speed miles per hour

Regulator closed

91
Mile | Post

90
Mile | Post

Speed miles per hour

This re-analysis of *Mallard's* record run was made in 1964, when *Mallard* joined the National collection at the former Clapham Museum, the precursor to today's National Railway Museum in York. NRM

Above: The Lincolnshire village of Little Bytham is dominated by the massive bulk of the East Coast Main Line structures and viaduct over which *Mallard* and other locomotives ran when setting their speed records. ROBIN JONES

Left: The village sign at Offord Cluny alongside the East Coast Main Line south of Huntingdon depicts *Mallard* as it appeared in LNER days. ROBIN JONES

OFFORD CLUNY

Mallard at Waterloo on June 22, 1948, during the Locomotive Exchanges which were held by the newly-nationalised British Railways that year is a bid to see if one 'Big Four' company's locomotives might perform as well if not better in another region. NRM

No. 60022 *Mallard* leaving London King's Cross with the Down 'Tees-Tyne' Pullman to Newcastle in 1955. NRM

Driver Bill Hoole leans from the cab of A4 No. 60034 *Lord Faringdon* waiting to move at Retford in the 1950s. Did he ever take an A4 down Stoke Bank at 132mph? ERIC TREACY

Mallard undergoing restoration to its 1938 condition in Doncaster Works in 1963. NRM

Mallard at a National Railway Museum press call after restoration, in June 1986. NRM

Mallard passing Crambe with the 'Scarborough Flier' in 1987. NRM

Right: The special 1988 Royal Mail stamp depicting *Mallard*. ROYAL MAIL

Mallard crosses the Nidd Viaduct at Knaresborough with a special for Royal Mail on May 6, 1988. 53A MODELS

To mark the 70th anniversary of the world steam speed record run, all four British-based A4s were lined up at the National Railway Museum in York on July 5, 2008. From left are *Union of South Africa*, *Sir Nigel Gresley*, *Bittern* and *Mallard*. NRM

The last time *Mallard* ran: it is seen topping Ais Gill summit while heading a circular tour from Eaglescliffe to York via the Settle and Carlisle line on August 27, 1988, after stalling at Birkett Common due to a build-up of ash in the smokebox. BRIAN SHARPE

On July 26-27, 2003, *Mallard* was displayed at the Doncaster Works 150 open weekend.

Sir Nigel Gresley the man with *Sir Nigel Gresley* the A4 Pacific named after him. NRM

Above: No. 60007 *Sir Nigel Gresley* departs Goathland with the 9.30am Grosmont-Pickering service on May 3, 2013, during the North Yorkshire Moors Railway's 40th anniversary gala. PHILIP BENHAM

Left: *Sir Nigel Gresley* leaving Doncaster with its post-war record-setting journey to King's Cross with a Stephenson Locomotive Society special on May 23, 1959. ERIC OLDHAM

Scarborough PE teacher Kelly Williams holds the Olympic Torch in front of *Sir Nigel Gresley* at the North Yorkshire Moors Railway's Pickering terminus on June 18, 2012 on its journey to the 2012 London Summer Olympic Games. NYMR

Fifteen minutes after sunrise on December 1, 2007, No. 60019 *Bittern* storms through Huntingdon on the East Coast Main Line with its first main line passenger train for 34 years, the Railway Touring Company's 'White Rose' from King's Cross to York. BRIAN SHARPE

As No. 4492 *Dominion of New Zealand* and driven by West Coast Railways' Dave Blair and fired by Chris Yates, *Bittern* — with two tenders — passes through platform 4 at Doncaster on the Down slow line with the 8.18am (additional) King's Cross to York special (1Z52) on July 9, 2011. DAVID INGHAM

New out of the box: No. 4488 *Union of South Africa* pictured on June 22, 1937. NRM

No. 60009 *Union of South Africa* departs from Perth on April 15, 2008, with the Railway Touring Company's 'North Briton' tour. BRIAN SHARPE

A Dufaycolour Stereoscopic transparency of No. 4496 *Golden Shuttle* (later renamed *Dwight D. Eisenhower*) at Wakefield Westgate. NRM

Above: No. 60008 *Dwight D. Eisenhower* is lifted aboard the United States Lines SS *American Planter* at Southampton Docks on April 27, 1964, after being handed over by none other than British Railways chairman Dr Richard Beeching, a name synonymous with the mass closures of unprofitable railway lines in the 1960s. THE RAILWAY MAGAZINE

Left: The bell presented by the Canadian Pacific Railway being fitted to No. 4489 on March 17, 1938. NRM

No. 60010 *Dominion of Canada* southbound at Edinburgh Waverley. NRM

Described at the time as "a line of grace, power and speed", the LNER's five new 'Dominion'-type streamlined A4s built to haul the 'Coronation' train from London to Edinburgh were lined up at King's Cross station for the first time on Monday, July 3, 1937, exactly a year before *Mallard* set its world speed record, From left are No. 4492 *Dominion of New Zealand*, No. 4490 *Empire of India*, No. 4489 *Dominion of Canada*, No. 4488 *Union of South Africa* and No. 4482 *Golden Eagle* ready for inspection by officials. NRM

It is not only *Dominion of Canada* that carried a North American bell in service on the main line. GWR 4-6-0 No. 6000 *King George V*, seen in the STEAM museum in Swindon, still carries the bell it was given during its visit to the US in 1927. ROBIN JONES

Andrew Goodman interviewed on camera in front of *Dwight D. Eisenhower* prior to its extraction from the Green Bay museum building. PAUL FULLER

No stranger to Pacifics: the transport of LNER A3 4-6-2 No. 4472 *Flying Scotsman* after its tour of Australia in the Eighties was arranged by Andrew Goodman. MOVERIGHT INTERNATIONAL

The tender of No. 60008 *Dwight D. Eisenhower* is slid across the floor of the Green Bay museum building past a US 'Big Boy', an example of the world's biggest locomotive type. NATIONAL RAILROAD MUSEUM

No. 60008 *Dwight D. Eisenhower* slowly being inched up the loading ramp at the Green Bay museum in Wisconsin.
PAUL FULLER

Dominion of Canada undergoes a trial run movement out of its Exporail home on July 14, 2012. PAUL FULLER

The rising sun turns the side of *Dominion of Canada* to gold on October 3, 2012, prior to it being unloaded from the cargo ship that brought it back across the Atlantic. ROBIN JONES

Back home: the newly-repatriated A4 pair complete with headboards lined up on the dockside at Liverpool on October 3, 2012. NRM

A Moveright International low loader takes *Dwight D. Eisenhower* from Liverpool to Shildon on the M58 on October 4, 2012. FRED KERR

Dominion of Canada being unloaded on to the rails in the Locomotion yard on October 3. LEANNE MANDALL

National Railway Museum director Steve Davies celebrated the arrival of *Dwight D. Eisenhower* and *Dominion of Canada* at Shildon with a bottle of champagne supplied by *Heritage Railway* and *The Railway Magazine*, which were both media partners in the repatriation of the pair. ROBIN JONES

The historic line-up of three consecutively-numbered A4s in British Railways Brunswick green at Locomotion on October 20, 2012: from left to right are Nos. 60008, 60009 and 60010. FRED KERR

How an A4 would have looked during the Second World War: *Mallard* in black undercoat. ROBIN JONES

Steve Davies, the man who organised the Great Gathering, beside the black *Mallard's* nameplate. NRM

New cabside lettering for *Mallard* gets the final touch. NRM

Steve Davies tests the newly unpacked ceremonial bell of *Dominion of Canada* on October 11, 2012. A small crowd of guests gathered as the bell was screwed into place. Steve then rang it – its monotonous chimes enchanting the onlookers. ROBIN JONES

Job done! Gleaming and magnificent in its 1960s livery, No. 60008 *Dwight D. Eisenhower* is placed on display in the Great Hall at York in February 2013 following its cosmetic restoration. ROBIN JONES

As good as new – back in its LNER identity of No. 4489, *Dominion of Canada* basks in the Shildon sunshine. LOCOMOTION

This remarkable photograph was taken at Cholsey at 5.30am on May 29, 2013. *Bittern* is seen storming through the station during its high-speed test run which set a new preservation-era official speed record of 91.5mph. BRIAN SHARPE

Great shades of *Mallard* 75 years before: *Bittern* shows just what a Gresley A4 can do as it speeds through Sandy in Bedfordshire with the 'Ebor Streak' on June 29, 2013. BRIAN SHARPE

Record setters: The 'Ebor Streak' train crew after arrival at York on June 29, 2013. ROBIN JONES

The sceptics said it would never happen – but all six A4s appeared together around the turntable in the Great Hall at York on July 3, 2013. ROBIN JONES

Tim Godfrey (left), grandson of A4 designer Sir Nigel Gresley, on the footplate of *Dominion of Canada* with the Canadian High Commissioner, Gordon Campbell, at the Great Gathering. JOHN TITLOW

Steve Davies, the man whose vision made the Great Gathering possible. JOE DICK

At 8am on July 3, 75 years after its world steam speed record, *Mallard* breaks through a banner to mark the start of the Great Gathering, as it is shunted into the Great Hall at the National Railway Museum to join its five surviving sisters. JOE DICK

After its triumphant entry into the Great Hall at 8am on July 3, *Mallard* stands on the turntable waiting to be shunted into position alongside its five surviving sisters and be reconnected to the dynamometer car which recorded its world steam record. KIPPA MATTHEWS/NRM

The opening days of the first Great Gathering in July 2013 saw crowds jostle to take pictures of their favourite A4s. Queues stretched around the museum on both sides of Leeman Road long before the doors opened at 10am at the start of the Great Gathering. On the opening day, 5000 visitors entered between 10am and 1pm – an attendance which would have delighted many heritage railways holding a gala event over several days. ROBIN JONES

Right: Giants Refreshed was a painting commissioned by the National Railway Museum from artist Jonathan Clay to mark the refurbishment of No. 60010 *Dominion of Canada* for Mallard 75. Styled after a Terence Cuneo original, this one it has a cat catching Cuneo's trademark mouse.

Right: Classic A4 line-up in a 1930s LNER art deco poster. NRM

Below: As part of the Mallard 75 celebrations, Doncaster Metropolitan Borough Council placed this giant floral tribute to one of Doncaster Works greatest products on town centre roundabout. DONCASTER MBC

ICH DIEN

No. 4464

CLASS   A4

Still steaming, A4
No.4464 *Bittern*
stands on the
turntable in the
National Railway
Museum's Great
Hall on July 22, 2013
carrying the Prince of
Wales' coat of arms.
ROBIN JONES

A steamy arrival: Prince Charles alights from the Royal Train inside the Great Hall of the National Railway Museum, with A4 *Bittern* in the background, around 10.15am on July 22, 2013. NRM

During his July 22, 2013, visit Prince Charles sounds *Mallard's* whistle, powered by an air compressor, signalling *Bittern* to leave the Great Hall. ROBIN JONES

Prince Charles and then National Railway Museum head Paul Kirkman alongside *Mallard*. NRM

Resplendent in the sunshine on September 8, 2013, *Mallard* stands on the newly-laid siding in the front of Grantham station, a few miles north of the place where it set an all-time world steam railway speed record of 126mph on July 3, 1938. ROBIN JONES

Approaching Grantham on September 4, 2013, *Mallard* passes the landmark of the town's St Wulfram's church for the first time since 1962. BRIAN SHARPE

On September 13, 2013, *Mallard* stands outside the erecting shop at Doncaster Works, possibly for the last time. Known as The Plant, the works was established by the Great Northern Railway in 1853, replacing the previous workshops in Boston and Peterborough. Until 1867 it only undertook repairs and maintenance. Among the ground-breaking locomotives the works produced were the Stirling Singles, the Ivatt Atlantics and the Gresley Pacifics, including A1/A3 No. 4472 *Flying Scotsman*, and the A4s. In 1957, the last of more than 2000 steam locomotives was built and, in 1962, carriage building at Doncaster also finished, but the works was modernised with the addition of a diesel locomotive repair shop. Under British Rail Engineering, new diesel shunters and 25kV electric locomotives were built, along with Class 56 and Class 58 diesel-electric locomotives. In early 2008 the main locomotive repair shop was demolished to make way for housing. BRIAN SHARPE

Left: *Mallard* basks in the sunshine at Barrow Hill Live on September 28, 2013. This scene can never be repeated, for the twin century-old 100ft chimneys of the adjacent brickworks in Campbell Drive, a popular backdrop for enthusiast photographers were blown up on December 12 that year. The brickworks had already been closed by owner the Phoenix Brick Company. ROBIN JONES

This picture was taken at 10am when the museum opened at the start of the Autumn Great Gathering on October 26. Within 10 minutes, the Great Hall was packed with visitors, and it remained that way for the rest of the day. ROBIN JONES

The three LNER garter blue A4s – *Bittern, Mallard* and *Dominion of Canada* – again lined up together. NRM

LNER goods guard Harry Croucher is fourth on the right in the now legendary picture of *Mallard's* crew after the record breaking run taken at Peterborough. Also pictured are fireman Thomas Bray, driver Joe Duddington and inspector Sam Jenkins. NRM

Julie Slater, granddaughter of world speed record 'mystery' guard Harry Croucher, in the cab of *Mallard* during the Autumn Great Gathering. NRM

The A4 drivers and firemen from King's Cross 'Top Shed' came together on the first day of the autumn Great Gathering. NRM

Former drivers and firemen from York shed at the NRM on October 26, 2013. NRM

During the Autumn Great Gathering, the museum's souvenir shop did a brisk trade in these attractive large ceramic *Mallard* tiles, priced £25 each. ROBIN JONES

Above: The Mallard 75 logo projected on to the wall of the Great Hall during the Locos In A Different Light contest. ROBIN JONES

Right: *Mallard*, illuminated by students from the University of South Wales, came third in the Locos In A Different Light competition inside the Great Hall. ROBIN JONES

No. 4464 *Bittern* accelerates towards 90mph past Bolton Percy just south of York on December 7, 2013. PHIL WATERFIELD

At home in the 'Cathedral of Steam': *Bittern* stands at King's Cross after arriving with the 'Capital Streak' on December 7, 2013. PAUL SIMPSON

It may not be 126mph, but the magic of A4 steam at high speed was relived as the 'Capital Streak' raced past the modern-day sign on Stoke Bank north of Essendine which marks *Mallard's* 1938 record. JOHN HILLIER

So that's why they call it a Streak... yards from the Whistle Top pub, in failing light, *Bittern* thunders across the A16 at Tallington level crossing with the 'Capital Streak' on December 7, 2013. ROBIN JONES

During the February, 2014 East Coast Giants event, Barrow Hill roundhouse's Alexa Stott unveils the plaque on *Bittern* which marks the locomotive's heritage-era steam speed record set on December 7, 2013. ROBIN JONES

A defining image not just of the preservation era but also the entire steam age: in the first of a series of £90-a-head evening photographic charters at Locomotion, organised on behalf of the museum by photographer Martin Creese, all six surviving A4s lined up: left to right are No. 60007 *Sir Nigel Gresley*, No. 60008 *Dwight D. Eisenhower*, No. 60009 *Union of South Africa*, No. 4489 *Dominion of Canada*; No. 4464 *Bittern* and No. 4468 *Mallard*. MARTIN CREESE

The afternoon of Wednesday, February 5, 2014, saw *Union of South Africa* towing *Mallard* from the National Railway Museum at York along the East Coast Main Line to the Locomotion museum for the Great Goodbye. STUART BROWN

Mallard being cleaned inside the Locomotion main building on February 6, 2014, the day after its arrival for the last of the three Great Gatherings. LOCOMOTION

An hour before the doors opened on a wet February 15, 2014, for the Great Goodbye, all six A4s are lined up in their public display positions on the Locomotion museum apron. ANTHONY COULLS

Hauling a rake of brakevans on the Locomotion running line, *Bittern* passes a Northern Rail Class 142 'Pacer' DMU set calling at adjacent Shildon station on the Bishop Auckland branch. Patronage of the branch services was so great at times during the Great Goodbye that it was described as akin to a Toyko commuter station in the rush hour. 'Pacers' have since followed the A4s into the pages of history, being withdrawn by national network operators in swathes during 2020, with many finding a new home on heritage railways. ROBIN JONES

It is 1937 all over again! The three surviving blue A4s lined up together at Locomotion on February 21, 2014. ROBIN JONES

Named after the speed record icon, Mallard David Elcoat is seen inside the cab of his namesake at Locomotion before the Great Goodbye. LOCOMOTION

Left: The final word: after Mallard 75 originator Steve Davies delivered his speech at the Great Goodbye gala dinner, he was presented with a framed Martin Creese picture of the six A4s' line-up from four nights previously, along with a special glass plaque from Mortons Media, Britain's biggest railway magazine publisher, by author and *Heritage Railway* editor Robin Jones, on behalf of both the magazine and sister title *The Railway Magazine* as a thank you gesture. JAMES SHUTTLEWORTH

The party is over: No. 60009 *Union of South Africa* propels its support coach and *Mallard* out of the Locomotion yard and on to the Bishop Auckland branch on Monday, February 24, 2014. ANTHONY COULLS

One A4 that will not be moving from County Durham, let alone going across the Atlantic, is this brick sculpture on the eastern outskirts of Darlington, a few miles from Locomotion. Named Train, it is the work of artist David Mach and was unveiled by Lord Palumbo of Walbrook on June 23, 1997. ROBIN JONES

Network Rail chairman Sir Peter Hendy unveils Hazel Reeves' bronze statue of Sir Nigel Gresley on the concourse of King's Cross station on April 5, 2016. LESLEY BENHAM

Beautifully restored to original 1937 condition: the art deco interior of Gresley Beavertail saloon No. 1719. DAVID MATHER/HORNBY

A4 No. 4468 *Mallard* in the Great Hall of the National Railway Museum on January 11, 2019. ROBIN JONES

LNER Beavertail observation car No. 1729, pictured inside the OneCollection museum in Margate alongside Class 55 Deltic D9016 *Gordon Highlanders.* DAVID MATHER/HORNBY

HORNBY
THE GREAT
GATHERING

№ 4468
CLASS   A4

Harrow rail crash, Automatic Warning Systems were fitted to all locomotives and No. 60009 received its apparatus on February 17, 1960, when a Stone-Smith type speed recorder was also fitted.

No. 60009 has been fitted with 14 boilers in its lifetime, the last being No. 29337 from No. 60023 *Golden Eagle* on November 6, 1963. It has had five tenders of two different types. The first was a 1928-pattern streamlined corridor tender, a rebuild of a tender fitted to a Class A1 or A3 Pacific and streamlined for fitting to an A4. It was later changed for a new-build streamlined corridor tender from 1948-1963. Currently, *Union of South Africa* is fitted with a 1928-pattern streamlined corridor tender, allowing the cab crew to be changed while the locomotive is hauling passenger trains. This tender was originally fitted to the Gresley experimental high-pressure No. 10000.

Union of South Africa pulled the last booked steam-hauled train from King's Cross on October 24, 1964. It was 20 minutes late through Grantham due to a broken rail at High Dyke. It was also the last locomotive to be overhauled at Doncaster while in service. It was withdrawn from traffic on June 1, 1966, after which it was sold into preservation. New owner and Scottish farmer John Cameron built his own line on which to run it, the Lochty Private Railway in Fife. Railway preservation was still in its comparative infancy when his line opened in 1967, more than a year before the end of BR main line steam. Predating the Strathspey and Bo'ness & Kinneil railways, it was Scotland's first passenger-carrying heritage line.

After hauling London-Edinburgh express trains for much of its working life, it was strange to suddenly find a locomotive of the calibre of an A4 working a short line barely a mile long on what was to all extents and purposes a private farm. The Lochty Private Railway was the sole remaining stub of the single-track East Fife Central Railway which ran for just over 14 miles from East Fife Central Junction on the Thornton Junction-Leven line to Lochty.

Constructed with the aim of tapping coal deposits in the area while also serving local farms, the East Fife Central Railway was taken over by the North British Railway in 1896, three years after it was authorised by Act of Parliament. Opening on August 18, 1898, it never had public passenger trains but ran services for miners prior to the collieries along its length closing in the 1930s. The line itself was closed by BR on August 1, 1964. Two years later, John Cameron bought Lochty Farm plus the topmost three quarters of a mile of the branch and the terminus station site.

Spring 1967 saw track from Glencraig Colliery near Lochgelly lifted and relaid at Lochty where a shed to house the mighty A4 was built. The nascent Lochty Private Railway was soon up and running and ready for the official opening on June 14 that year when No. 60009, which, following preservation, had worked the last steam special in Scotland in 1967, hauled its first train on the short farm line, later extended to a new terminus at Knightsward. The A4 ran on the mainly volunteer-run railway on Sunday afternoons for six years before it returned to the main line two years after BR agreed to lift its steam ban.

Two industrial tank engines, Bagnall 0-6-0ST No. 2759 of 1944 *Wemyss Private Railway No. 16* and Peckett 0-4-0ST No. 1376 of 1915 *British Aluminium Co. No. 1* from Burntisland, were brought in to take over services on the line which was far more appropriate to their size. Supporting volunteer group the Fife Railway Preservation Group built up its own collection of industrial steam and diesel shunters, rolling stock and signalling equipment while recovering redundant track at various sites on the East Coast for use at Lochty.

John Cameron eventually decided that he wanted to use the site for other purposes and closed the railway in 1992. By this time, the Kingdom of Fife Railway Preservation Society had been established as a successor to the Fife Railway Preservation Group and launched a search for alternative accommodation for its locomotives and rolling stock. Most of it went into storage in 1994 at Scottish Power's Methil power station and a local haulier's yard pending the acquisition of a new 20-acre site, with the move funded by local authority grants. The society aims to open a railway heritage centre at Methil.

Following the end of the British Rail steam ban, in January 1973 two routes were allocated in Scotland for the running of steam-special trains. *Union of South Africa* headed the first such special, on May 5 that year, and hauled its nine-coach trains at speeds of up to 60mph over the Edinburgh to Dundee main line.

Leaving Lochty in 1973, No. 60009 was first based in the former goods shed at Kirkcaldy. It was later relocated to the goods shed at Markinch where it remained until May 1994 with the exception of two years which were spent in a shed in the yard at nearby Thornton. Since then it has been one of the most consistent main line registered steam engines, still in the ownership of John Cameron. It has accumulated the highest mileage of any locomotive in the class.

Due to the international public disgust at the continuation of apartheid during the 1980s and early 1990s, No. 60009 carried *Osprey* nameplates during this time. In May 1994 it left Markinch for the last time on a low loader bound for the Severn Valley Railway where repairs were to be undertaken in the Bridgnorth workshops. Its route took it over the Forth Road Bridge and in doing so it became the only steam loco to cross both the Forth Bridge and the adjacent Forth Road Bridge.

On October 29, 1994, it appropriately hauled the first steam train into King's Cross for 30 years on a railtour from Peterborough, under the banner of the 'Elizabethan', making more East Coast Main Line history, or rather carrying on from where it had left off in 1964. It was fitted with on-train monitoring recorder equipment in early 2007.

Union of South Africa's most recent overhaul, at pop mogul Pete Waterman's LNWR workshops at the Crewe Heritage Centre, beginning in 2010, was said to have cost nearly £1 million. It returned to the main line on July 22, 2012, and continues to give magnificent service to destinations all over the country. However, John Cameron does not plan to overhaul it again, but instead place it on static display in a new visitor centre he aims to open in Fife.

DWIGHT D. EISENHOWER

When No. 4496 entered traffic on September 4, 1937, it was named *Golden Shuttle* and painted in LNER garter blue with stainless steel trim on the base of the valances and tender. The numbers and LNER lettering on the tender were also stainless steel, and it had a single chimney and side valances covering the wheels. This livery design was also used on the A4s that were named after countries on the 'Coronation' service in order to match the rolling stock.

It was to have been named *Sparrow Hawk*, but that name was later used on No. 4463. No. 4496 was painted wartime black on January 30, 1942, when the valances were removed, with the livery modified on March 12, 1943, the tender lettering reduced to NE.

The garter blue livery was reapplied on September 25, 1945, and the name changed to that of *Dwight D. Eisenhower*, the Supreme Commander of Allied Forces during the latter part of the Second World War — breaking the tradition of renaming engines after LNER officials. The name was covered up until February 1946. It had been intended that Eisenhower himself would attend an official unveiling, but it could not be arranged. It was also renumbered 8 on November 23, 1946.

After Nationalisation, it became No. 60008 on October 29, 1948. British Railways' dark blue livery with black and white lining was applied on June 14, 1950, and replaced with Brunswick green on November 9, 1951. Experimental Automatic Train Control equipment was installed on June 23, 1950. A double chimney and Kylchap double blastpipe was fitted on August 20, 1958. A Smith-Stone type speed indicator was installed on June 30, 1960.

Golden Shuttle, which was allocated to work the 'West Riding Limited', was first allocated to Doncaster during September 20-29, 1937. Then it was moved to King's Cross until December 4, 1939, when it was reallocated to Grantham. On June 4, 1950, it was reallocated back to King's Cross. Another move to Grantham came on April 7, 1957, with it again returning to King's Cross on September 15, 1957. Its final allocation was New England shed in Peterborough from June 16, 1963, four days before it was withdrawn from service.

Dwight D. Eisenhower had 11 boilers in its career, including No. 29312 from No. 60010 *Dominion of Canada* fitted on August 20, 1958. Its last replacement boiler was No. 29335 from 60019 *Bittern*, fitted on May 17, 1962. It had two tenders, No. 5651 from new and No. 5671 from April 1, 1957. On October 4, 1962, *Dwight D. Eisenhower* hauled a special train from

Stratford in east London to York, after being specially cleaned by King's Cross 'Top Shed' staff.

In the 1950s, as steam disappeared from US railroads earlier than in Britain, a National Railroad Museum was established in Green Bay, Wisconsin, by the Great Lakes, north of Chicago. A chance conversation between a Mrs Kovachek, who was on holiday from Yorkshire, and a man she thought was the museum's gardener resulted in No. 60008 ending up in the US. The 'gardener' turned out to be the chairman of the museum's board, Harold E Fuller. When he found out that there was a locomotive named *Dwight D. Eisenhower* in the UK, he became determined to add it to the collection. British Railways, however, would not sell it to him.

General Eisenhower had strong connections with Britain's railways as there had been two military command trains in Britain during the run-up to D-Day, which were for the future president's exclusive use. These trains, mainly of GWR stock and codenamed Alive, included two LNER Gresley coaches, which were the general's favourites. When No. 60008 was withdrawn, BR finally agreed to donate the engine and the two LNER coaches used by General Eisenhower to the Green Bay museum. There they were displayed together for many years from 1964.

It is only in recent years that research on both sides of the Atlantic has led its US custodians to realise that Dwight D. Eisenhower would almost certainly never have hauled either of its namesake's military trains in Britain during the Second World War. Still in BR green livery, as cosmetically restored at Doncaster Works on July 19, 1963, prior to export it was shipped to the US, arriving in New York Harbour on May 11, 1964. It was taken by rail to the museum later that month.

In October 1990 it was moved to Abilene, Kansas, for the celebrations of the centenary of Eisenhower's birth. The move both ways was carried out as a special train at slow speed, since the locomotive and two cars from the command train used the British vacuum-braking system which is incompatible with the American air-braked trains.

In 2000, *Dwight D. Eisenhower* was given pride of place in a new museum building at Green Bay, still with the Gresley coaches attached and standing alongside Union Pacific articulated 4-8-8-4 'Big-Boy' No. 4017, the idea being that a member of the world's fastest class of steam locomotives stands next to the world's biggest.

DOMINION OF CANADA

Outshopped from Doncaster Works on May 4, 1937, No.4489 was originally to have been named *Buzzard*, but entered traffic as *Woodcock*. For its first fortnight in service it ran in works grey with green-painted wheels, but was taken back inside 'The Plant' and by the end of May had been repainted into LNER garter blue livery.

At that point, it was renamed *Dominion of Canada* because it had been chosen to haul the 'Coronation' streamlined express. The coat of arms of Canada appeared on the side of the cab, with the worksplates moved inside and a Canadian Pacific Railroad-type bell mounted ahead of the single chimney. The bell was steam operated and was used in service. The locomotive was also fitted with a Canadian Pacific Railway whistle.

As a livery variation for the five 'Coronation' engines named after British Commonwealth nations, a stainless steel strip ran along the bottom of the valances and tender and the numbers and letters of the locomotive and tender were also stainless steel. No. 4489 achieved 109.5mph when running down Stoke Bank in 1937. After later being damaged in a collision at Hatfield, it was repaired at Doncaster Works between January 31 and March 18, 1939. It was repainted into wartime black on February 21, 1942, when the side valances were removed and the livery was modified with the basic NE carried on the tender on November 27, 1943.

It was renumbered 10 on May 10, 1946, and on October 27, 1948, became British Railways No. 60010. Garter blue livery was reapplied on November 20, 1947, and British Railways' dark blue livery with black and white lining was applied on September 29, 1950. It was repainted into Brunswick green on May 8, 1952.

The Canadian coats of arms worn on the side of the cabs were removed on April 8, 1949, but the worksplates were not moved back. The whistle was replaced with a standard chime whistle in 1949 and the bell was removed when the chimney was replaced with a Kylchap double blastpipe and chimney on December 27, 1957.

First allocated to King's Cross from new, *Dominion of Canada* was reallocated to Grantham on April 7, 1957. It was switched back to King's Cross on September 15 that year. When 'Top Shed' closed, it went to New England and its final allocation was to Aberdeen on October 20, 1963, to be used along with other A4s displaced by 'Deltics' from the East Coast Main Line. There, it was mainly used for the three-hour Aberdeen to Glasgow express service.

No. 60010 was officially withdrawn at Darlington shed on May 29, 1965, having not been repaired since May 12. The locomotive had 11 boilers during its career, including No. 9018 from *Bittern*, fitted on April 8, 1949, and finally No. 27970 from *Sir Nigel Gresley*, installed on December 5, 1962. It had six tenders.

No. 60010 was marked in Darlington's records as "for sale to be scrapped" on July 5, 1965. Its chimney was removed for use on either No. 60004 *William Whitelaw* or No. 60024 *Kingfisher*, with both in the works at the same time. No. 60010 was then moved behind Darlington Motive Power Depot and left at the end of a weed-choked siding, all but forgotten about.

As a schoolboy, Graham Horricks watched A4s on the 'Tees-Thames' service run past his school at Yarm, near Saltburn-by-the-Sea, and remembers the day when No. 60010 was taken back into Darlington Works to be refurbished after BR agreed to donate it to the Canadian Railroad Historical Association along with its bell which had been in storage. After Darlington Motive Power Depot was closed on March 26, 1966, No. 60010 was moved to Crewe Works for further cosmetic restoration and shipping to Canada.

"People have said that it was refurbished at Crewe, but they just finished it off," said Graham. "Most of the work was done at Darlington."

No. 60010 was shipped to Canada aboard the MV *Beaverbrook* after it was formally presented to Geoffrey Murray, Acting High Commissioner for Canada, at Royal Victoria Dock, London, in April 1967. It was preserved at Exporail, the Canadian Railway Museum, at Delson/Saint-Constant, Quebec, near Montreal. The bell was shipped out with No. 60010 but was not refitted due to the double chimney. Over the years, there have been several bids made to buy either No. 60008 *Dwight D. Eisenhower* or No. 60010 from their North American museum owners so that they could be returned to Britain and restored to running order, but all have been rebuffed.

CHAPTER 10

Newsflash!

T HE NATIONAL Railway Museum at York announced in late 2009 that a new director had been appointed. Steve Davies, who had been director of the Museum of Science and Industry in Manchester for less than 18 months, took over the following February. The former British Army colonel, who had been Army Chief of Staff Headquarters 2nd Division, overseeing the activities of 250 central staff and 10,000 troops across the north of England and Scotland, was a railwayman through and through, and the ideal candidate to succeed the long-serving Andrew Scott.

While serving with the Army in Sierra Leone, in his spare time he transformed a warehouse of decaying railway artefacts, including locomotives and carriages from the Queen's train used during her visit in 1961, into a new Sierra Leone National Railway Museum, initially paying staff wages from his own pocket. That museum was officially opened in 2005 by the President of Sierra Leone and Andrew Scott.

Speaking about his appointment at York, he said: "This is a once-in-a-lifetime opportunity that I really could not afford to miss. The NRM is the world's pre-eminent railway museum and a British national treasure. It is critically important to the UK."

He seized the opportunity with both hands. With an eye on the horizon, he saw something very special would have to be arranged for 2013 to celebrate the 75th anniversary of Britain's greatest steam moment, *Mallard's* 126mph triumph down Stoke Bank. The obvious course of action would be to resteam *Mallard*, but where would be the commercial benefit, with three other examples already running on the main line? There again, maybe all four could be brought together for a line-up... but that had already been done at the museum in the summer of 2008.

In August 2011, *Heritage Railway* magazine's website received a huge number of hits when it was the first to break the story that Steve and his NRM colleagues had been in talks for six months with the hitherto obstinate museums in North America which had both stoutly refused to entertain any notion of exiled No. 60008 *Dwight D. Eisenhower* or No. 60010 *Dominion of Canada* returning to the UK. The same stance was taken over the Canadian museum's LBSCR 'Terrier' 0-6-0T No. 54 *Waddon*. Neither of the expatriate A4s nor *Waddon* have ever been steamed in preservation.

In any case, No. 60008 was effectively bricked up inside a museum hall at Green Bay, Wisconsin, so even if its owners were willing the prospect of getting it out would be daunting. Steve threw a new offer on the table. The NRM would borrow both locomotives for two years — so a unique line-up of all six surviving A4s could be staged — and then return them. Both, especially No. 60010, were in need of new coats of paint, and they would be cosmetically restored as part of the deal. No. 60010 would be taken back to its 1938 condition, in which it would be able to carry the Canadian National Railroad bell which the country had presented to it when new, and which was a unique feature among the 35 A4s.

After Steve made a series of visits to North America, both museums surprised everyone by agreeing to the deal, providing it was shown to be feasible — and so the seeds of Mallard 75, which would centre around three world headline-grabbing Great Gatherings of the six A4s, were firmly planted. The story was featured as a world exclusive in *Heritage Railway* issue 154. The museums had tried to keep the repatriation project confidential while talks were ongoing but from the start it was obvious that if Steve managed to pull the repatriation off, it would create one of the biggest moments in the history of global railway preservation.

When *Heritage Railway* published the story, there were many who said that the temporary repatriation would never happen. They were to be proved wrong, but it took more than a year of meticulous fine-detail planning, covering every base and negotiating sponsorship deals, before the pair would be loaded on board a ship at the Nova Scotia port of Halifax and brought home, opening the page on a ground-breaking new chapter in the world history of Railway preservation.

THAT SPECIAL RELATIONSHIP

Since the Second World War, Britain has been said to have had a special relationship with the USA. Indeed, such a relationship goes back much further, if you take the global railway revolution into account. In 1828, the British-built *Stourbridge Lion* not only then became the first locomotive to be operated in the United States, but was also one of the first locomotives to operate outside the UK.

Following its withdrawal after the conversion of the last of Brunel's 7ft 0¼in broad gauge to standard gauge the year before, Iron Duke 4-2-2 *Lord of the Isles* was exhibited at the Chicago World's Fair in 1893, and at Earls Court, London in 1897. Later, the GWR preserved it at Swindon, but disgracefully, while chief mechanical engineer George Jackson Churchward was away on holiday in January 1906, it was cut up on the orders of none other than William Stanier, who went on to design the great LMS Pacifics of the 1930s. Only the driving wheels survive.

Had *Dwight D. Eisenhower* and *Dominion of Canada* not found new homes in North America, a similar fate would almost certainly have befallen them, and Britain therefore owes both museums a debt of gratitude. Two months after GWR 4-6-0 No. 6000 *King George V* emerged from Swindon Works in June 1927, it visited the USA to star in the Baltimore & Ohio Railroad's centenary celebrations. While there, it was presented with a souvenir bell and a plaque, and these became a trademark of the locomotive, one of three Kings to survive, and which returned steam to the UK main line in 1971.

The LMS sent Royal Scot 4-6-2 No. 6100 *Royal Scot* to the Century of Progress Exposition Chicago in 1933. It toured both the USA and Canada, covering more than 11,000 miles with a train of LMS carriages. However, it was not all that it seemed. The locomotive was not the first member of the class which appeared in 1927, but No. 6152 *The King's Dragoon Guardsman*, built three years later and which had exchanged identities with No. 6100. It too was given special commemorative plates fixed below its nameplates. After the 'new' No. 6100 returned to Britain, the identities were never exchanged again.

Streamlined Stanier Princess Coronation Pacific No. 6229 *Duchess of Hamilton* exchanged identities with No. 6220 *Coronation* in 1939 and was sent to the USA along with carriages from the 'Coronation Scot' train to attend the New York World's Fair. The locomotive was shipped back in 1942, and the identities of the pair were exchanged again the following year. *Coronation* did not survive into preservation, but *Hamilton* did, in its rebuilt form. Its streamlined casing was rebuilt by Tyseley Locomotive Works in 2008, and it was placed on display in the Great Hall at the NRM.

In 1969-70, Alan Pegler, who had bought A3 Pacific No. 4472 *Flying Scotsman* from British Railways in 1963, took it along with several coaches on a tour of North America to promote British industry. It was fitted with a cowcatcher, bell, buckeye couplings, American-style whistle, air brakes and high-intensity headlamp. The trip ran into severe financial difficulties however, and *Scotsman* found itself marooned in California. Pegler was left bankrupt in 1972, returning home by working his passage as a ship's entertainer.

Businessman and rail enthusiast Sir William McAlpine, who had his own private railway at his Fawley Hill home in Buckinghamshire, came to the rescue in 1973 by paying £25,000 for the stranded engine direct from the finance company. It returned from San Francisco via the Panama Canal in February of that year before being overhauled at Derby Works and making a comeback on what is today branded as the Dartmouth Steam Railway between Paignton and Kingswear.

The first main line locomotive to be bought by a private individual visited Railfair '91 at Sacramento. Great Northern Railway 0-6-0ST No. 1247, a former King's Cross pilot which had been saved by the late Captain Bill Smith, came face-to-face with Sharp Stewart Highland Railway-type 0-4-4T *Dunrobin*, which was subsequently repatriated to Beamish Museum in County Durham.

CHAPTER 11

Bringing two A4s back across the Atlantic

EXPORTING TWO A4s to North America was a fairly simple task back in the Sixties. You took them by rail to the nearest port, loaded them onto a ship, and watched them sail into the sunset. It was up to their new American and Canadian owners as to what happened to them on the far side of the Atlantic. However, getting them back was slightly more difficult.

The first hurdle had been overcome by National Railway Museum director Steve Davies – persuading the US National Railroad Museum at Green Bay in Wisconsin and the Exporail museum in Montreal to release their prize exhibits on loan in exchange for refurbishment – but this was indeed only the first hurdle.

Getting the engines to a point where they could even be moved at all was the next. The NRM turned to a man with a record second to none for tracking steam locomotives overseas and bringing them back to the UK against all odds – haulier Andrew Goodman of Moveright International. An enthusiast since his early childhood, young Andrew went with his dad and uncle to Saltley sheds in Birmingham at the age of four, and stood on the turntable looking up at "great big steam engines" in the form of Stanier 8Fs and BR Standard 9Fs.

A year later, he was taken with his dad, uncle and two friends to Dai Woodham's legendary scrapyard at Barry, after having earlier stopped to inspect two yards at Newport when he saw a Britannia, No. 70026 *Polar Star*, earmarked for the cutter's torch. At Barry, he walked along the lines of condemned locomotives and clambered on top of the boilers of the GWR 'Kings'. He promised himself — "one day I will come back and buy one of these engines".

Sixteen years later, Andrew was studying law at Cardiff University. Barry became a second home for him at weekends, making frequent trips to take photographs, although the number of engines diminished as more were saved by the heritage railway movement. One day he was driving home to the Midlands when he decided to take the old country route from Cheltenham via Winchcombe and Broadway instead of the M5. He drove up to the roundabout at Toddington, and noticed some activity in the derelict station there.

Following a derailment at Chicken Curve north of Winchcombe in 1976, British Rail decided to rid itself of the by-then freight-only Stratford-upon-Avon to Cheltenham route, and despite local protests, ripped up the 28 miles of track in 1979. The Gloucestershire Warwickshire Railway was formed to reopen the route, and chose the derelict station at Toddington as its base. The first weekend that its volunteers moved on to the site to clear it, the station was devoid of platforms and the station building was being used as a store for the adjacent garden centre. This was the day that young Andrew drove in to see what was going on.

THE START OF A MOVING CAREER

He started chatting to a couple of volunteers, who later would become firm friends, and was hooked. This chance encounter started a life-long association with the heritage line which continues to this day. Andrew kept his vow to return to Barry that September, when he and a group of like-minded people bought GWR 4-6-0 No. 5952 *Cogan Hall*, and moved it to Toddington, just after No. 7821 *Ditcheat Manor*, No. 7828 *Odney Manor* and 2-8-0 No. 2807 had arrived for restoration, along with two industrial steam locomotives and a diesel.

At the Gloucestershire Warwickshire Railway in 1982, Andrew became involved with the purchase of three Western Region Class 14 diesel hydraulics which had seen latter-day service in industry at Corby steelworks. They had to be moved to Toddington, so Andrew organised the task himself. Equipped with only a desk, a telephone and a fax machine, as a middle man he arranged for outside hauliers to do the job.

That was the start of Moveright International — heavy haulage and abnormal load specialists — which celebrates its 40th anniversary in 2022. Later in 1982, an opportunity arose for Andrew to buy Bagnall 0-6-0ST No. 2655 of 1941 *Byfield No. 2*, along with two friends. The locomotive was operational and had a boiler ticket, but was buried at the back of its owner's factory in Hinckley. The factory needed space for expansion, so the engine was up for sale. Andrew, his uncle and friends, had to jack it up, move it sideways, turn it through 90-degrees twice and then pulled it up a slope. The whole procedure took four days.

Byfield No. 2, a veteran of the ironstone quarries of Northamptonshire and Oxfordshire, was taken to Toddington where vacuum brakes and steam heating equipment were fitted. It was used on short trains on the line, but was withdrawn when the boiler ticket expired in the mid-1990s, by which time it was considered too small for the expanding railway. Bought by the Plym Valley Railway, it moved to that line's Marsh Mills site in September 2002. At this time, Andrew was working for Norwich Union in Birmingham, and the transport business was very much still a spare time affair, although it was beginning to grow.

RAF officer Andy Bryne, a member of the group restoring GWR 2-8-0 No. 2807, bought GWR 2-8-0T No. 4277 from Barry in 1987 and moved it to Toddington. Andrew was asked to help extract it, an awkward task as it was trapped at the end of a line of rusting hulks behind Bulleid 'West Country' light Pacific No. 34046 *Braunton*. As no hydraulic winch was available, Andrew reached agreement with a Mr Jones of Newport to turn up in his 1915 Foden steam lorry. It winched Braunton on to a trailer, allowing it to be moved to another road, and then Andrew was able to move No. 4277. It was taken to Toddington and restored. It was sold to the Dartmouth Steam Railway in 2008 and named *Hercules*.

Altogether, Andrew extracted 12 locomotives from Woodham's scrapyard, including the last to leave – GWR prairie No. 5553 – this engine passing into the ownership of Pete Waterman. By that time Andrew had changed his day job and was working for an insurance broker in Birmingham. He was asked to look after British Rail Staff Association clubs all over the country, a dream job. "Whenever I visited one, we spent an hour talking about insurance and two talking about railways. I met some marvellous characters," he said. This task carried on for about five years.

TRIUMPH FROM DISASTER

The flooded River Ness washed away the old Victorian railway bridge linking Inverness to the Far North Line to Wick and Thurso and the Kyle of Lochalsh branch in February 1989.

A train packed with passengers had passed over the bridge about 40 minutes before it was washed away. It seemed like the death knell for a line which had been earmarked for closure in the Beeching Report a quarter of a century before, but ScotRail decided to rebuild the bridge and keep it open. Andrew won the contract to move the locomotives and rolling stock between Inverness and Invergordon while the construction work was taking place.

He was running a road shuttle of stock, including Class 37s, Class 156 units and coaches over two six-week periods, one in the early spring and another in October.

For Andrew and his business, this was the turning point. After the ScotRail contract, he was asked by locomotive owners Harry Needle and John Wade to move a collection of around 40 shunters from a site in Meadowhall, Sheffield, that they were being forced to vacate. His boss at the insurance brokers listened sympathetically, and agreed to let him have a year out to concentrate on his haulage business, leaving the door open for him to return if it did not work out.

Andrew never went back. Setting up full time on his own, one of the most unusual of his early jobs was to move a Grade II listed granary barn from the Watership Down home of composer Andrew Lloyd Webber near Newbury in Berkshire. The Viables Craft Centre at Basingstoke had just lost an historic barn after it burned down and Baron Lloyd Webber offered to give them a replacement which stood in his back garden. As it was listed, advice was sought from the Department of the Environment, which refused permission for the building to be taken apart. So it had to be moved in one piece. Andrew came up with a scheme to move it using a specially constructed steel frame, which could be lifted by a crane.

"Andrew Lloyd Webber's mother-in-law was going ballistic because she did not want the crane on his front drive," he said. "We moved the barn complete, and this set us up for other jobs moving similar types of structures."

TURKISH REPATRIATION

Fellow enthusiast Mike Hoskins told Andrew in 1989 that he had bought a Stanier 8F in Turkey, one of the many examples that ended up in regular post-war service in the Middle East after being built in the UK as part of the war effort, and needed to get it home. By then, Andrew certainly had the necessary expertise.

As part of the deal, they went on a railtour, flying from Heathrow to Istanbul and on to Ankara, and then taking an overnight coach to the Black Sea resort of Samsun. Woken up by the 4am calling to prayer, they boarded a special steam train for a week's tour of the Turkish rail system. He and his fellow travellers used up all their rolls of film on the first day, and when they arrived in Sivas, went to look late at night for a shop to buy some more. They found one next to a cafe, but it was closed, and asked the cafe owner when it would open again.

The cafe owner drove off in his battered old Fiat van, emitting clouds of smoke, and 20 minutes later came back with the shop owner, who agreed to open despite the time of day. He was rewarded by the group buying his entire stock of film. "It is amazing what you can do talking pidgin English and the signs," said Andrew.

At the Sivas steam depot, they saw a number of 8Fs. "Never did I think that for one moment I would one day be going back to recover two of them."

At one point, the railtour went close to the Syrian border, where some runpasts were staged. "All of a sudden there was a load of click click clicks. We were suddenly surrounded by Turkish army conscripts. Their captain had trained at Sandhurst and we told him we were railway enthusiasts. He said it was a very dangerous area and gave us a military escort out."

After that, North British 2-8-2 No. 46185 headed the train up into the Taurus Mountains, a mountain range in southern Turkey, dividing the Mediterranean coastal region from the central Anatolian Plateau. After climbing for a day, the train ended up at Konya where the purchased 8F had been brought down from Izmir after overhaul and pushed into the half roundhouse, breaking the main bearing on the turntable in the process. The party had to wait for a week while one man helped by a diesel jacked up the turntable and changed the bearing.

The party lived in a railwaymen's hostel for a week, and had been warned not to venture out if they could avoid it, and if they did so, tell anyone they were Australians or Canadians, and definitely not British or American. Konya was still ruled by mullahs and Salman Rushdie's The Satanic Verses had just been published, lighting a tinderbox in the Muslim world, with threats of reprisals. The 8F was marshalled into a half-mile-long freight train, but in the middle. It departed at 5am, and the buyers riding on its footplate were chilled to the bone in the freezing mountain temperatures.

After a few hours, the party managed to persuade the Turkish crew to remarshall the train, so the 8F was behind the diesel. In the cab of the diesel, they took turns to crouch down on the floor next to the heater to get warm. At 8am, the end of this leg of the journey was reached and the train remarshalled again. Andrew recounted: "What followed was the railway journey of a lifetime because we came down the Taurus Mountains through the night and it was absolutely spectacular. The diesel on the front was trying not to brake, and the whole train rolled through ravines, across viaducts and through tunnels. A shower of sparks flew off the wheels of the diesel every time the driver touched his brakes. It was just like November 5."

The 8F, Turkish State Railways No. 45160, had been exported as a kit of parts to Turkey in 1940, and was now coming home complete. It was sent to Mersin, the main port in southern Turkey to be loaded onto a ship for the homeward journey. Horror of horrors! The shipping agent at the port said it could not be loaded before the ship sailed, because it was Ramadan, and the stevedores refused to work. Eventually, a deal was struck with the stevedores. For two bottles of whisky and 400 Marlborough, they agreed to work on the Saturday morning, and so the party was able to load the 8F over the weekend. Left absolutely shattered by the Monday morning, they flew back, while the ship with the 8F on board sailed to Immingham and then the Swanage Railway, its first restoration base.

Back in the UK, it ran for a time in Turkish livery but was later rebuilt, and has been running as LMS No. 8476, a Swindon-built example of the class, on where else but the Gloucestershire Warwickshire Railway. However, it would not be Andrew's last venture overseas prior to embarking on his A4 mission to America. Far from it.

STOPPED AT GUNPOINT

Among the many railway locomotives imported from the USA during the Second World War were the United States Army Transportation Corps 0-6-0T 'dock tanks', 14 of which entered the Southern Railway fleet in 1946, and of which four survive in preservation.

During and immediately after the war, up to 400 of these locomotives were deployed across Europe and many entered regular service in France, Greece, Hungary, Turkey, Czechoslovakia and Yugoslavia.

The authorities in communist Yugoslavia were so impressed with the design that, over several years, 'pirate' copies were made in their own workshops, based on the US design but incorporating modern improvements. They became Class 62 and some members were still active in the country during the 1990s. A group of British enthusiasts, who would later form Project 62, decided to buy one in the form of No. 62-669. This engine had been built as recently as 1960 by Duro Dakovic of Slavonski Brod in Croatia, and was found at the Store Steelworks near Ljubljana. It had been made redundant after only 25,000 miles in service.

Andrew was hired as haulier to bring No. 62-669 to Britain. The operation involved the locomotive being divided at the steelworks into the boiler and the chassis so that the lorry could negotiate the Alpine road tunnels. When Andrew and his team crossed the border from Trieste in December 1990, they immediately noticed that something was up. The streets were packed with military vehicles such as tanks and half-tracks. It was the year that Slovenia began its journey to independence. The following Sunday, two days before Christmas, a referendum on independence was to be held. There were fears that if there was a 'no' vote, civil war could break out.

Constitutional amendments introduced parliamentary democracy in September 1989 and on March 7, 1990, the Slovenian Assembly changed the official name of the state to the Republic of Slovenia. On December 23, 1990, more than 88% of the electorate voted for a sovereign and independent Slovenia, which became reality on June 25 the following year, immediately leading to the Ten Day War with parent Yugoslavia. Eventually, the EU recognised Slovenia on January 15, 1992. Its independence had been achieved with much less carnage than other states of the disintegrating Yugoslavia.

The British party drove through the night to the steelworks, where an interpreter handed Andrew an envelope of documents, insisting that despite his knowledge otherwise, no export licence was needed. The locomotive components were classed as scrap metal. Driving to the north Yugoslavia border, the team encountered a tailback of trucks stretching for more than 12 miles nose to tail. Eventually, they reached the frontier post, where a customs guard looked at the documents given to Andrew by the interpreter, and said: "Papers no good." Pointing to the locomotive, he said: "National monument!"

An argument ensued, with Andrew insisting the papers were good.

"He was quite insistent, with me giving him the papers and him handing back," said Andrew. "This carried on for 20 minutes as other truck drivers crowded around banging our truck and waving their arms because they could not get out. Eventually the guy took the gun out of his holster and stuck the gun in my face and said 'papers no good — you go back!'

"We turned round in no-man's-land and the pilot car took us back to Maribor. It turned out that all I had been given was an invoice for scrap metal."

Eventually, the Belgrade government issued release forms for the loco-motive and the papers were stamped at the border post before they were allowed into Austria. More problems then arose, this time in 'friendly' western European countries. The Austrian border guard told them that they could not drive on Austrian roads with the lorry after 5pm on Fridays, and would have to park up for the weekend. Andrew reached agreement for them to drive to the next town where there was a truck park.

"We must have missed the turning for the truck park because we kept going," he said. "And we drove across Austria and reached the German border at 7pm."

There, a border guard told them they could not drive on German roads after 10am Friday until 6am on Monday. Again, they agreed to drive to the next truck park. "We must have missed the turning for the truck park because we kept going," said Andrew.

Eventually they rolled into Zeebrugge, only to find that a strike had been going on for several weeks with no ships being loaded. They were told there was a chance of boarding a ship at Ostend — and reached it with only seconds to spare. "We literally drove onto the ship just before the back door came up," said Andrew.

At Dover, HM Customs demanded payment on VAT and excise duty on 40 tons of scrap metal, and despite it being a heritage engine, would not budge. Andrew's trailers were impounded over Christmas and the new year until the buyers stumped up the cash. No. 62-669 was restored to running order, and was given the British Railways number 300075, in line with the sequence of the real US dock tanks.

ADVENTURES IN SOUTH AFRICA

Further jobs abroad led Moveright International to South Africa. South African Railways (SAR) 3ft 6in gauge 25NC 4-8-4 No. 3405 of 1958 was imported for static display at the Buckinghamshire Railway Centre, while three 2ft gauge NGG16s and two NGG15s were brought to Britain for intended use on an abortive project at Robin Hood's Bay in Yorkshire, most of them ending up at the Welsh Highland Railway.

An expedition to recover Glasgow-built SAR 15F 4-8-2 No. 3007 started out as a 12-day trip and ended up taking four weeks. Firstly, despite earlier bookings, there were problems in persuading SAR to transport No. 3007 from the redundant steam depot at Bloemfontein to Durban, or finding a road haulier with the right equipment to do the job.

A road haulier was found but then the sign at the entrance to the yard had to be dismantled so the 15F could leave on a low loader. This done, police promptly blocked the movement, saying it was unsafe, and the team were back to square one. Eventually, SAR found a locomotive, crew and 10 flat cars, and agreed to move the engine to Durban. A 500-mile trip on secondary lines via Lesotho took five days. Deep in the middle of winter, Andrew and his team nearly froze to death on the footplate. Someone provided them with a brazier. "It was only that brazier that kept us alive that night, and we huddled around it burning on the footplate. It was so cold you could not get the grease onto the rods."

At Durban, the team found that the crane on the booked ship was inadequate, so the shipping company had to honour its contract by hiring the harbour's floating crane at £20,000 for a day. Then it was found that no longitudinal top beam for lifting the locomotive on to the ship was available despite one having been ordered. Eventually, one was located along with two essential cross spreaders, but it was discovered that no thin bottom spreader existed anywhere in South Africa. However, a kindly Glaswegian agreed to fabricate the 50-ton lifting beam within three days.

Andrew told the shipping line that there was no suitable heavy equipment to lift the engine at Immingham Docks, but officials did not believe him. Eventually, the company dumped it on the dockside at Hamburg. Andrew was understandably furious, and after a week of threatening legal action, the shipping company chartered a coaster to take the 15F to… Immingham, where Andrew needed to hire a 1000-ton crane to lift it onto the dockside. Finally, the 15F arrived in Glasgow, where it now holds pride of place in the locomotive hall at the new Riverside Museum of Transport.

Moveright International returned to Sivas in Turkey in December 2010 to repatriate two more 8Fs, to be overhauled and rebuilt to British outline. No. 45170, which was bought privately, was displayed at Locomotion and then moved to the North Norfolk Railway as a long-term restoration project. Sister TDCC No. 45166 was acquired by the Churchill 8F Group, owner of No. 8274/WD341, which had been successfully returned to steam. It decided to sell it in order to finance another project, but there were no UK buyers.

An offer from Municipality of Be'er Sheva in Israel was forthcoming and accepted. The derelict locomotive was wanted as the principle exhibit in the Be'er Sheva regional railway heritage centre in Be'er Sheva's historic Old Town. No. WD341 was to be restored to represent Israel Railways No. 70414 (originally No. WD414), in 1958 condition on static display at the old Be'er Sheva station, a declared National Heritage Site. The locomotive was moved from Barry to Southampton Docks on Thursday, November 22, 2012 by Moveright International, arriving at Southampton Docks the following morning, and was loaded on to Mafi shipping trailers later that day. The locomotive was subsequently shipped from Southampton to the port of Ashdod by Grimaldi Lines on the *Grande Europa*. The restoration work was completed and the engine is now on display.

BRINGING THE A4S BACK HOME

Moveright International first worked for the National Railway Museum when the firm took its working *Rocket* replica to Japan for an exhibition. Andrew was back again in 1991, carrying a redundant Shinkansen bullet train power car donated by the Japanese to the York museum. The Japanese went as far as painting the ship which took it on the two-day first leg of the voyage, from Kobe to Yokohama, in the train's livery for what was deemed to be a very special occasion. From Japan, a Wallenius Lines vessel took the car to Southampton. The bullet car has, since its arrival, been one of the most popular exhibits at York.

Andrew's business brought him to Canada in 2011 to repatriate Sharp Stewart 0-4-4T *Dunrobin*, which had been built in 1885 for the 4th Duke of Sutherland. Also coming home was a four-wheel saloon built for the duke to run behind *Dunrobin*. Bought for $15,000 from their bankrupted Canadian owner by the Government of British Columbia in 1965, they became exhibits at Fort Steele Heritage Town, where *Dunrobin* was last steamed in 2005. In 2010, both were declared surplus to requirements, and in January 2011, it was announced that they had been bought by Beamish Museum.

The locomotive and coach arrived home on May 16, 2011, *Dunrobin* initially being taken to the Severn Valley Railway's Bridgnorth Works. While Andrew was in Canada, he went to the Exporail museum to see if it was physically possible to extract No. 60010 *Dominion of Canada*, and then visited the US National Railroad Museum at Green Bay, Wisconsin, to ascertain if the same could be done with No. 60008 *Dwight D. Eisenhower*.

Steve Davies was already toying with the idea of borrowing the pair and had asked Andrew for his opinion on the feasibility of the notion. Andrew returned again in May 2011 with an asbestos specialist to see if there were likely to be any problems in that field, and after it was ruled there were none, he went back yet again in late October. A fourth visit was made in early 2012 to finalise the deal, and made a fifth one in the summer with Steve. At long last, the start of one of the biggest adventures in preservation was about to begin.

Andrew left his home in Evesham on Sunday, July 15, 2012, and arrived in Canada the following day. He said: "It was particularly poignant, as when *Dwight D. Eisenhower* was taken from Crewe Works to Southampton in 1964 for export to the US, it passed through Evesham."

The movement was due to begin four days later, but the first of many hitches came to light when a shocked Moveright International team was told that the necessary railcars were away on a wind farm project in Tennessee; they were the only five of that type available in North America and would not be available until August 13.

SIDEWAYS SHUFFLE FOR AN A4

Andrew had done his sums long beforehand regarding the extraction of No. 60008 from Green Bay. The delicate operation of moving the engine, tender first, began on Saturday, July 28. The A4 had to be gingerly moved sideways on a 'sled' to manoeuvre it around two of the museum's internal pillars — with only 3in leeway on either side. Andrew had come up with the ingenious method of removing No. 60008 from the museum building by sliding it sideways on to an exhibition road two roads away. It was then pulled out of the museum building in the traditional way.

The 'locking in' of No. 60008 had been one of the major reasons given as to why it could not be moved out on loan. But now No. 60008 finally emerged into the scorching sunshine of a 100-degrees Fahrenheit day — its tender having been moved out overnight. The engine and its tender were then placed on flat wagons at the museum and taken out via its main line connection. The train carrying *Dwight D. Eisenhower* departed on August 4, and took a route normally reserved for local stopping trains, rather than fast straight-through services, due to it being considered as an 'excessive dimension' load because of its weight.

From Canadian National's Green Bay yard, the train ran to Fon du Lac (Wisconsin) and on to Joliet near Chicago, where it was held up for several days. Problem after problem compounded the move from there on. Firstly, Canadian National could not find a route from Chicago to move the locomotive and tender, which eventually 'disappeared' in Illinois. Andrew and his team had to spend five days trying to relocate it and struck lucky only when someone sent him an email with a photograph of the pair in Kirk yard. Then US customs managed to lose the document authorising the use of Moveright's lifting gear.

Running through Kirk (Indiana) and Battle Creek (Michigan), the train finally crossed the border into Canada, at Sarnia, on August 11. From there, the train ran on to Concord (Toronto), Montreal, Quebec City and Moncton (New Brunswick) before arriving at Rockingham Yard outside Halifax Docks on the evening of August 19.

There, No. 60008 was unloaded, and the same two wagons which brought the engine and tender were sent to Montreal to collect its sister locomotive. These wagons had to be used because they were the only wagons available that had been passed for carrying the weight.

Dominion of Canada's move was also problematic. Exporail lies on a Canadian Pacific (CP) line, so Canadian National (CN) had to first hand over the cars to carry the A4 to CP. No. 60010 was taken from the museum before CN realised that it had not obtained four special wagons needed to provide braking force for the consist to Halifax. So the engine had to go back to the museum for another week.

HOME AND DRY

Finally, after a journey lasting weeks and a month of delays, both A4s were able to set sail aboard the Atlantic Container Line cargo ship from Halifax, Nova Scotia, on September 25, 2012, reaching Liverpool a week later. It was a 6am start on October 3 for the select group of media who had been invited to witness the A4s being unloaded from the ship, including representatives of *The Railway Magazine* and *Heritage Railway*.

There were many who said it would never happen. But at last there was living proof it had. However, it was only when the pair were seen basking in the rays of the dawn sunlight on the dockside that it was confirmed – everyone's dreams had finally come true. Steve Davies said: "We wanted to do something really special to mark the 75th anniversary of *Mallard* breaking the world speed record and what could be more spectacular than an international family reunion? When these mighty machines were exported across the Atlantic in the Sixties, no one thought they would ever come back; now they are finally here.

"The sheer scale of this transcontinental project to move these loco-motives back to home soil was immense and it is testament to the vision and expertise of all those involved. Our thanks go to them for making this historic homecoming happen. What is marvellous about the pair is that they are like time capsules. They are exactly as they would have run on British Railways, without any modifications for modern running. This is their real historical value."

Gary Hodgson, managing director of Peel Ports Mersey, said: "When the NRM approached us and asked if we would be able to help facilitate this reunion we were only too pleased to be able to offer our port services and logistics expertise. Railways and ports have traditionally had a very close relationship, and they continue to do so. It is a real privilege for the Port of Liverpool to be able to welcome these extraordinary machines back to the UK. They are a wonderful reminder of our country's great capacity for engineering excellence, and a heritage we should all be proud of."

The Port of Liverpool worked closely with shipping line Atlantic Container Line, which specialises in carrying oversized cargo, to co-ordinate the arrival of the locomotives from Nova Scotia. Once unloaded at Liverpool, it was not simply a case of immediately taking the locomotives onwards to their intended destination, the National Railway Museum's outreach station of Locomotion museum at Shildon, where they were immediately placed on public display. First, customs paperwork had to be completed before they could be released from Liverpool Freeport.

The A4s had to make the journey one by one since only a single low-loader was available. The series of delays had meant that Moveright International only had one available that week, so it had to take *Dwight D. Eisenhower* to Shildon on the Thursday afternoon, before returning to Liverpool the following day to collect *Dominion of Canada*, which departed at 4am on the Saturday. The route took the A4s along the M58 out of Liverpool, and then up the M6 to Cumbria. From there, the lorries took the A66 across the Pennines.

In the days of steam, no A4 ever ventured across Stainmore Summit, at 1370ft the highest point on the trans-Pennine South Durham & Lancashire Union Railway. It was also the highest point on the UK national rail network until the legendary Stainmore route was closed in 1962. The location was marked by a famous cast iron sign which is now preserved at Head of Steam, the Darlington Railway Museum. From there onwards, it was a downhill run to Shildon.

THE FIRST LINE-UP

As soon as the repatriated pair were displayed at Locomotion, to which entry is free of charge, the response from the public was overwhelming; crowds flocked to gaze at two locomotives they thought would never again appear in Britain. It was indeed appropriate that the A4 pair should go first of all to Shildon, widely regarded as the 'cradle of the railways'. While Cornishman Richard Trevithick invented the steam railway locomotive, it was the likes of northerners George and Robert Stephenson who honed it to perfection. The vast coal deposits around Shildon led to George Stephenson engineering the Stockton & Darlington Railway, the world's first public steam-operated line, which opened in 1825.

The railway established its workshops at Shildon in 1825, and the population grew to around 9000. The town was the birthplace of Timothy Hackworth and steam locomotives such as Rainhill Trials entrant *Sans Pareil* were built there. Daniel Adamson, Hackworth's apprentice and a renowned engineer in his own right, was also born in Shildon. Shildon's crucial part in the history of steam railway technology — which reached dizzy new heights with *Mallard's* record-breaking run down Stoke Bank — is celebrated at Locomotion.

During their initial stay at the museum, a special photographic charter event was arranged for enthusiasts. For what might be the last time ever, three British Railways Brunswick green-liveried A4s stood side by side outside the museum. Event organiser 30742 Charters arranged for No. 60009 *Union of South Africa* to run to the museum to join the repatriated pair.

Over the evening of October 19-20, 2012, all three were lined up outside the museum. There, scenes which would once have been commonplace at sheds such as King's Cross, New England at Peterborough and Grantham were replicated under floodlighting, and all in honour of absent sister *Mallard*. Unlike the museum setting of the Great Hall at York, the yard at Locomotion allows locomotives to be lined up on several roads outside, making such recreations appear authentic.

CHAPTER 12

Repainting the 'I' in iconic

T HE GROUND-BREAKING project to stage the line-up of all six surviving A4s was never going to be anything less than an extremely special occasion, one to be viewed from way beyond the shores of Britain and North America. As far as Steve Davies and his team of organisers were concerned, it went without saying that the locomotives all had to look their very best for the big occasion.

Suffice to say, it could be argued that the transatlantic journey of the North American pair was not concluded until they received cosmetic makeovers, a core part of the deal under which they were borrowed. *Mallard's* garter blue paintwork had been looking somewhat tired, so in the summer of 2012, the opportunity for cosmetic restoration was taken. Early August saw No. 4468 given a fresh black undercoat. It was moved out of the National Railway Museum's Great Hall into the sunshine where it could be photographed in 'wartime black'. Afterwards, the Bury-based team from Heritage Painting, then a relatively new company which had built up a superb track record of repainting classic steam locomotives, began to apply a brand new coat of the LNER's striking garter blue livery which is a trademark of *Mallard*. The firm then carried out the cosmetic restoration of No. 60008 *Dwight D. Eisenhower* after it was brought to the museum by low loader in the autumn.

The promised cosmetic restoration of No. 60008 was finished in January 2013, and once the gloss was dry, it was moved from the museum workshops into the Great Hall to proudly take its place alongside *Mallard*. The Great Gathering had begun to gather.

Ian Drewitt of Heritage Painting said at the time: "It is a tremendous honour to think that our workmanship will be exhibited in the USA and Canada when the locomotives return. Not only did we paint *Mallard* and *Dwight D. Eisenhower*, but we also hand painted the new crest for *Dominion of Canada* and the boiler barrel of *Union of South Africa*."

Dominion of Canada presented the more daunting task. Under the loan deal, No. 60010 was to be restored to its as-built condition complete with valances and garter blue paint. That task was largely contracted out to Darlington-based M-Machine, a company which has built up a specialist business not in repainting legendary locomotives but in restoring classic Mini cars. In many ways, therefore, a wheel had turned full circle; for as we saw earlier, it was a Bugatti racing car which had sown the seeds of the inspiration for the streamlining of the Italian's diesel railcars and then Gresley's A4s.

Ian Matthews of M-Machine first became involved in repainting railway engines in 1986, when he tackled a small electric shunter located at Darlington. A coach restorer at the Eden Valley Railway, in 2012 he repainted the new £3 million A1 Peppercorn Pacific No. 60163 *Tornado* into British Railways express passenger blue livery before returning it to LNER apple green in 2015. He was also at the centre of operations in 2011 to briefly transform *Bittern* into scrapped sister No. 4492 *Dominion of New Zealand* in 1930s style in garter blue livery and complete with new valances on behalf of owner Jeremy Hosking. Fitting the valances to *Dominion of Canada* was a joint operation between M-Machine and the restoration team at Locomotion. M-Machine's Peter Horwood made the new chimney.

A large dent in the front of the casing – sustained when the locomotive was involved in a shunting accident at the Montreal museum – also had to be ironed out. Ian said: "Much has been said about the peeling paint on *Dominion of Canada* but in reality it was simply life expired and needed to be removed. Similarly, all the filler in the bodywork had turned dusty and had to come out. Underneath that, we found all the repairs that British Railways had done.

"We had to rub the paintwork down to bare metal. The whole restoration job took between January and the middle of May and I was working up to 80 hours on it some weeks. I was physically wrecked. The real reward comes when you see people photographing the finished product and enjoying it. We are proud to have become part of the locomotive's history."

The Friends of the National Railway Museum donated £50,000 to cover the lion's share of the cosmetic overhaul of the repatriated pair. The estimated cost of restoring No. 60008 was £22,000 and that of *Dominion of Canada* £37,000. The figures covered all the work carried out by contractors and the costs associated with buying the necessary parts and equipment for the work being undertaken by the museum workshop team; and included the supply of paint, asbestos remediation to make the vehicles safe for sanding and painting, and the removing and refitting of the motion and bodywork repairs.

The paint applied to the refurbished trio itself has a legacy that goes back way beyond the days of the LNER. The company which supplied the paint not only provided it when Gresley's 'Streaks' were built in the first place, but also for Locomotion No. 1 which ran on the Stockton & Darlington Railway, the world's first public steam railway, and no less than Stephenson's *Rocket* itself back in the dawn of the steam era.

Established in 1775, T&R Williamson of Ripon, Yorkshire, is believed to be the oldest family-operated paint manufacturer still in existence anywhere in the world. The Williamson family, of Scottish and French descent, are recorded in the Ripon area as early as 1738 involved as horse-drawn carriage builders. Various family members were renowned artists and their link to the pre-Raphaelite era exists today in the form of the Williamson gallery in Liverpool.

Around the time of the Jacobite uprising in 1745, it is recorded that a French refugee stumbled into Ripon's market square. He was speaking in his mother tongue and not understood so Daniel Williamson, who was known to speak French, was summoned to deal with this visitor. Daniel took the refugee under his wing and offered him lodgings. The French man rewarded Daniel's kindness with secrets, knowledge and the ingredients to produce varnish and lacquers. Varnish and lacquer production started around the mid-1700s with Daniel at the helm. A cottage industry emerged and varnish was sold at 30 shillings per gallon in the 1760s — carried to customers across the country by stagecoach and carriage. Thomas and Robert Williamson, Daniel's sons, formally established the company in 1775.

The firm is still providing paint for heritage steam locomotives today, as well as diesel and electric traction owned by the post-privatisation main line operators. Its paint was used when the Royal Train was revamped for the wedding of Prince William and Catherine Middleton in 2011.

The steam age came and went and T&R Williamson is still here. Railways will almost certainly still be using its products long into the future. The work carried out by Heritage Painting and M-Machine with the T & R Williamson products ensured that *Dominion of Canada* and *Dwight D. Eisenhower* will remain star exhibits back in their respective countries for many years to come. The same applies to *Mallard* in the UK. With *Sir Nigel Gresley*, *Bittern* and *Union of South Africa* running on the main line in 2012, the museum decided early on that there was little point in going to the trouble and additional expense of resteaming *Mallard* for its 75th anniversary.

However, who knows what might happen when the centenary of its record-breaking run eventually comes around in 2038?

CHAPTER 13

The 21st century record breaker

W HAT COULD be more befitting of the 75th anniversary celebrations for a world steam record than the setting of another
record or two? That is exactly what happened when multi-millionaire locomotive owner Jeremy Hosking's main line operational arm,
Locomotive Services Limited, decided to arrange three very special trips
to mark the occasion.

Special dispensation from Network Rail was sought to run his A4 No. 4464
Bittern at 90mph on three passenger-carrying trips over the East Coast Main
Line. The modern-day speed limit for steam locomotives on the UK national
network is 75mph, but what could be a better reason for a one-off bending
of the rules than celebrating the anniversary of a great British achievement?

On April 24, 2013, Locomotive Services announced the dates for the
three runs. The first trip, the 'Ebor Streak', was scheduled to run north
from King's Cross to York on Saturday, June 29, picking up at Potters Bar,
beyond which 66 miles of route had been identified as suitable for running
at speeds in excess of 75mph. The train would also be a positioning move
to allow *Bittern* to run from York station to the adjacent National Railway
Museum, where it would be the final piece in the Great Gathering line-up
jigsaw five days later, with electric traction on the return leg.

The second trip, 'Tyne-Tees Streak', was arranged for July 19. From York, *Bittern* was scheduled to head the train to Newcastle-upon-Tyne and back, the tour starting from Bristol behind a diesel. The last trip, 'Capital Streak', was scheduled between King's Cross and York on July 27. Passengers on all three trains were to be entered into a draw to win the special commemorative whistle carried by No. 4464 *Bittern* for these runs.

The winning ticket was planned to be drawn by Jeremy as it descended Stoke Bank on July 27. However, to make it happen, a test run would first have to take place. Before the trips were announced, *Bittern,* by then running again as such following its short-lived spell masquerading as *Dominion of New Zealand,* had been tucked away in its shed at Southall, receiving months of attention and fine tuning in readiness for its 90mph test run.

The run, with DB Schenker driver Don Clarke at the regulator of *Bittern,* was set for the early hours of Wednesday, May 29, on a stretch of Isambard Kingdom Brunel's original Great Western Railway main line between Southall and Reading, with 90mph recorded both ways and 91.5mph at one point during the 15-mile stretch between Didcot East Junction and Tilehurst East Junction.

The test train (5Z64) comprised *Bittern's* support coach and seven Mk.1/2 vehicles, with a total loading of around 250 tons. It was booked off Southall depot at one minute past midnight – the outward journey included run-rounds in Southall goods loop between 00.11 and 00.31 then shortly afterwards, Hanwell goods loop between 00.34 and 01.04. The Hanwell loop was used due to a main line block on the Southall loop. Reading was booked to be passed at 01.42, three minutes before the 90mph test began on the Down main at Tilehurst East Junction, ending at Didcot.

On arrival at Didcot station, the coaches were stabled in platform 5 while *Bittern* entered the Didcot Railway Centre yard for turning and servicing. Returning at 05.23, two minutes early, the train (5Z65) was routed on Up fast for a second 90mph run. It passed Reading at 05.43, two minutes ahead of schedule, passing Twyford at 05.49 right time, passing Slough three minutes early at 05.58, passing Airport Junction at 06.68 right time, arriving at Southall West Junction at 06.13.

Placed into Southall Goods loop, *Bittern* returned to Southall depot at 06.37, right time. The engine had set a new official record for a high-speed steam running in the preservation era. Accordingly, the green light was given for it to head the three passenger-carrying trips... and the A4 went on to break its own new record! On June 29, hauling the 'Ebor Streak', *Bittern* departed King's Cross with 10 coaches on a loading of 350 tons.

Given the road, Don Clarke accelerated the A4 from a standing start at the pick-up stop of Potters Bars to average 71.4mph to a pathing stop north of Huntingdon, the speed over this authorised section peaking at 90.5mph.

Bittern reached 70mph just five miles out of Potters Bar on a rising gradient and took just three minutes between Biggleswade and Sandy at 88/90mph. On the fast line, the A4 overtook a stopping train but was halted to give the stopper precedence on to the two-track section across Holme Fen. Slowing to a stand for a brief water stop at Holme Junction, *Bittern* was again opened up and diverted onto the fast line.

It accelerated through Peterborough ahead of a late-running Edinburgh train, and further maintained 72-79mph at Stoke summit, the train four minutes early, and five through Grantham, which was passed at around 79mph. The second 90mph authorised section began at Barkston, but beyond Peascliffe Tunnel, the A4 was opened up and let fly. The high point of the trip came at Balderton crossing south of Newark-on-Trent where the A4 and train reached its top speed of 92.5mph, beating its test run best, before heading through Northgate station and slowing at Crow Park.

No. 4464 stopped for water at Babworth loop, just short of Doncaster. Control allowed an early restart in front of other late-running trains, but after accelerating away through Doncaster at 70mph and passing Temple Hirst Junction at around 90mph, the train, now well ahead of schedule, was brought to a stop by signals at Hambleton North Junction. Nevertheless, the 'Ebor Streak' was five minutes early at Colton Junction prior to running into York nine minutes ahead of time.

Among the 262 passengers on board the train — 89% of seats had been sold — was former *Flying Scotsman* chief engineer Roland Kennington, the man who oversaw *Bittern's* rebuild. Roland spent the entire journey between King's Cross and York with Peter Townend, King's Cross (34A) shedmaster from 1956-1961, and described the three sections of 90mph running as "superb". He enthused: "I was delighted to receive an invitation, and I thought it an absolutely excellent run. It went very well indeed, and I enjoyed it."

Peter also mentioned his enjoyment at running through Peterborough and topping Stoke Bank on the fast road and Doncaster on the middle road. "The engine didn't seem to be working hard, and I am pleased I didn't miss the trip — it brought back a lot of memories. It's fantastic and just goes to prove the capabilities of an A4. Marvellous, just marvellous — but only what they did in the old days, of course!"

Traction inspector Gareth Jones said: "*Bittern* loved it. She would have done 100mph if we'd let her... easily!"

Passenger Paul Sprackland from Bristol said: "I never thought I'd live to travel at 90mph behind steam again... not in Britain anyway."

After arrival at York, *Bittern* and its support coach were uncoupled and moved into the National Railway Museum's north yard, all set to take their places around the Great Hall turntable for the Great Gathering.

SUMMARY OF ACCEPTED RAIL STEAM SPEED RECORDS

MPH	Locomotive	Railway	Date
	Trevithick's first steam locomotive	N/A	February 21, 1804
15	*Locomotion No. 1*	Stockton & Darlington, UK	1825
30	*Rocket*	Liverpool & Manchester Railway, UK	1830
60	*Antelope*	Boston & Maine RR, US	1848
78	*Great Britain*	GWR (broad gauge), UK	1850
81.8	No. 41	Bristol & Exeter Railway (broad gauge), UK	June 1854
82	Empire State Express No. 999	US	May 10, 1893
90	No. 790 *Hardwicke*	LNWR, UK	August 22-23, 1895
102.3	No. 3440 *City of Truro* 'Ocean Mails Express'	GWR UK	May 9, 1904
115	E2 No. 7002	Pennsylvania RR, US	June 11, 1905
103.5	F6 No. 6402	Milwaukee Road, US	July 20, 1934
100	A1 No. 4472 *Flying Scotsman*	LNER, UK	November 30, 1934
104.7	A3 No. 2750 *Papyrus*	LNER, UK	March 5, 1935
112.5	Class A No. 2	Milwaukee Road, US	May 8, 1935
112	No. 2509 *Silver Link*	LNER, UK	September 29, 1935
113	No. 2512 *Silver Fox*	LNER, UK	August 27, 1936
114	No. 6220 *Coronation*	LMS, UK	June 29, 1937
124.52	No. 05002	Germany	May 11, 1936
125.88	No. 4468 *Mallard*	LNER, UK	July 3, 1938
113.3	No. 18201	Germany	October 1972
92.5	No. 4464 *Bittern*	ECML, UK	June 29, 2013 (preservation era record)

CHAPTER 14

Mallard 75: the first Great Gathering

'OH TO be a football fan on cup final day,' ran the old saying. True, but football fans can experience the euphoria of the FA Cup final at Wembley, or at least watch it on TV, once a year. However, what about being a railway enthusiast on the day that all six surviving LNER A4 Pacifics are reunited for the first time in the preservation era, and in showpiece condition too? That has happened just once in a lifetime, and may never be repeated.

Or maybe, at the opposite end of the spectrum, how about being an ordinary member of the public who doesn't care about railways either way, but just wants to savour a truly great landmark for Britain, when a footplate crew comprising ordinary locomen did much to restore the pride to our nation still reeling from the effects of the Great Depression by snatching the world steam speed record from Germany so we could keep it for all time?

The big event – the Great Gathering at the National Railway Museum in York – kicked off on July 3, 2013, the exact 75th anniversary of the fabled run down Stoke Bank. Admission to the event was free, with visitors being asked for a voluntary donation of just £3 a head. As recounted in the previous chapter, the final piece of the jigsaw fell into place on the afternoon of Saturday, June 29, when A4 No. 4464 *Bittern* arrived at York with the 'Ebor Streak' from King's Cross. After detaching from the train and running with its support coach into the museum's north yard, it became the last of the six to arrive.

On the evening of Tuesday, July 2, in front of camera crews from the BBC's The One Show, the visiting A4s were shunted into their pre-determined positions around the turntable in the Great Hall.

Back in the BBC studio, international rock megastar and renowned model railway enthusiast Rod Stewart pulled a lever which saw *Bittern* turned on the turntable to face its road for the Great Gathering. One of the first VIP guests to arrive for a special press preview at 7am the following day was none other than Steve Davies, who dreamed up the idea of borrowing the two A4s from North America to make it happen. On September 16 the year before, he had resigned his post as the museum director to pursue a new private sector venture, creating an inland surfing resort in the Conway Valley, being replaced by acting director Paul Kirkman, who joined on secondment from the Department for Culture, Media & Sport where he was Head of Arts and Creative Industries. "It's just wonderful to see it," said Steve.

Nothing was going to stop him seeing the fruits of his NRM team's endeavours — in short nothing less than a seminal moment in the history of British transport heritage.

Indeed, amassing all six was nothing less than a world-class piece of museumship. The net result was the railway equivalent of equally ground-breaking exhibitions such as The Treasures of Tutankhamun tour, which ran from 1972-81 after being first shown at the British Museum in London in 1972.

Earlier in 2013, the NRM issued a statement which said that the cost to the museum of staging the Great Gathering was around £25,000, before a number of other sponsorship deals had been agreed. Thanks to the generosity of sponsors on both sides of the Atlantic, that figure was less than a third of what the expense might have been.

In the weeks prior to the Great Gathering, the Science Museum Group, of which it is part, had expressed fears that one of its northern museums — possible the NRM — might have to close if the Government went ahead with a feared 10% budget cut for 2015/16. Those fears were allayed by Chancellor George Osborne when he announced his spending review in June 2013, after public protest.

However, while it would certainly be a brave or foolish Government that would ever close the NRM, the affair did bring into question exactly what the public wants from its museums. Do we want dry, dusty showcases where exhibits are not changed for years at a time or should we have havens of education and inspiration where a little cash might have to be splashed from time to time? There is no doubt that the Great Gathering fell firmly into the latter category.

There have been several pinnacle points in the history of railway preservation, where 'missions impossible' have been accomplished with spectacular results: the building of the Ffestiniog Railway's Llyn Ystradau deviation, the rebuilding of the partially scrapped No. 71000 *Duke of Gloucester* in which its original faults were ironed out, the building of an all-new A1 Peppercorn Pacific, No. 60163 *Tornado* from scratch, the reopening of the complete Welsh Highland Railway from Porthmadog to Caernarfon, the reconnection of the Bluebell Railway to the national network at East Grinstead on March 23, 2013... and now the Great Gathering is up there with all of these and more.

On that opening day, around 7000 visitors entered the Great Hall to see the shining six in place, and that was on a Wednesday when most potential visitors are still at work. Steam aficionados from all over the world, including Australia, Canada, the USA and beyond, amassed to celebrate *Mallard's* historic achievement. Travelling the farthest was Neil Waterland, who made a 25,000-mile round trip from Norfolk Island in the South Pacific especially for the event. He said: "I wanted to come over and see all the A4s together as since an early age, with a very influential father, I have been interested in all parts of the British Rail network, but the A4s are the ones that I love the most.

"The last time I was in England, 1989, my dad took me to the National

Railway Museum and I made a beeline straight for *Mallard*. During that visit to the UK we went on many a rail trip around the UK network and had more than one visit to the National Railway Museum. When I heard of the two expat A4s heading back to home soil I started making travel plans. As we live on a small island out in the South Pacific Ocean, which is only 8km by 5km so there's no train service, it means I have to fly to Auckland in New Zealand (one hour and 40 minutes with a seven-hour layover) then on to the UK via Los Angeles — 28 hours all in one go, but I know it's going to be worth every kilometre. All up I worked it out to be a 41,500km round trip and that's returning via Brisbane."

The event, of course, was also attended by senior representatives of the National Railroad Museum in Green Bay, USA, and Exporail in Montreal, Canada.

At 8am, *Mallard* sounded its trademark chime whistle before being shunted by the museum's Class 08 diesel shunter into the Great Hall from the yard outside and on to the turntable, before it was positioned alongside its sister locomotives *Sir Nigel Gresley, Dwight D. Eisenhower, Union of South Africa, Bittern* and *Dominion of Canada*.

A fanfare played by the York Railway Institute Brass Band marked *Mallard's* arrival into the Great Hall and signalled that the Great Gathering, the centrepiece of the *Mallard* 75 celebrations, was complete. Paul Kirkman opened the proceedings with his boyhood reminiscences of the star exhibit. He said: "*Mallard* is very special to me personally. Like so many children, it was the engine that my grandfather pointed out to me when I came to visit as a boy, and it was the first memory of the museum that I sought out when I was lucky enough to find myself in this fantastic job.

"Seventy-five years ago to this day, this mighty machine raced down Stoke Bank near Grantham at the incredible speed of 126mph. That placed a permanent marker on the international timeline for British technological excellence, and it's a record still held today. Not only was it a marvellous feat of engineering but it was also a triumph of British design. *Mallard's* technical ability is surpassed only by its beauty. It has earned its place in the hearts of millions and to me sums up everything great about British innovation: both our vision to be the best and our ability to achieve it.

"It was driven by Joe Duddington, a bit of a daredevil by all accounts, and fired by Tommy Bray, whose reputation for coal shovelling like his life depended on it meant that they were the dream team on the footplate. We have just been lucky enough to witness an international family reunion to mark the occasion. Particular thanks go to Exporail, the Canadian Railway Museum and the National Railroad Museum, Wisconsin, for letting us repatriate their A4s. Representatives from both museums are here today to witness their star exhibits' moment of glory — Jacqueline Frank and Dan Liedtke from the National Railroad Museum and Stephen Cheasley and Marie-Claude Reid from Exporail.

"Although I would love to take personal credit for this amazing sight which has drawn people from all over the world, I think it is only fair that I acknowledge the vision of former director of the NRM, Steve Davies, who is here today. Steve — I hope you are enjoying *Mallard* and her sisters together again and that we have successfully delivered your dream and the dream of rail enthusiasts across the globe."

Canada's High Commissioner in the United Kingdom, Gordon Campbell, formally unveiled No. 4464 in its original livery, and from the cab rang the bell which his country had presented to the LNER for use on the locomotive in 1937. Back then, the commissioner of the time was joined by Sir Nigel Gresley on the footplate during the original dedication. Completing a circle, this time round the commissioner was joined by Gresley's grandson Tim Godfrey.

Tim said: "I think it's great to see all these beautiful locomotives so beautifully kept by the NRM and the two from across the Atlantic which have been restored back to their former glory.

"Seventy-five years ago, *Mallard* came out of the works in Doncaster in the same month I was born in 1938. All I can say is *Mallard* looks a lot better than I do at 75."

He said that the appeal of *Mallard* and sister A4s was down to them being "brilliant performers designed for speed, efficiency, comfort and everything else" and the fact that aerodynamic lines, sculpted in a wind tunnel, are still influencing modern train designers.

Marie-Claude Reid, executive director general of Exporail, said: "*Dominion of Canada* looks amazing and we have watched its painstaking restoration every step of the way. We are thrilled to be loaning our treasured locomotive to the National Railway Museum to help the British people mark 75 years since *Mallard* broke the world speed record in style, but we look forward to its return and displaying it alongside the Royal Hudson where you can walk underneath it."

Jacqueline D Frank, executive director at the National Railroad Museum, said: "It's fantastic to see our locomotive surrounded by its surviving class members at this national and international celebration."

Retired locoman Ron Birch, 80, who regularly drove *Mallard*, said that in his day he would get 165 ton steam trains running at three-figure speeds. He said: "I've worked on diesel but there's nothing like steam and the Gresley A4 locos were the best of them all. These were the race-horses — they had very light feet. You only had to open them and they were off — but the brakes weren't very good. Each had its own personality."

Anthony Coulls, senior curator of railway vehicles at the NRM, added: "Bringing the collection to the widest possible audience is what it's all about, and this Great Gathering, a fortnight-long exhibition celebrating British engineering genius and showcasing all six survivors of the A4 class, is the stuff that dreams are made of. *Mallard's* record was the pinnacle of steam and it was the swansong because these locomotives, within two years, were hauling troop trains.

"It's special because of what it did on that day in July 1938, but for 20 years after it just settled down to being just another steam engine. By the end of their time, the A4s were dirty, they were unkempt and the glamour had gone. *Mallard* carved its place in posterity in 1938, so it was always assured that something good would happen to it. It is a Thirties icon. It's not just an icon of the railways — it's an icon of style. It's like nothing else."

A compressor supplied by manufacturer Thorite enabled *Mallard's* iconic whistle to sound once more, and it also drove the motor to ring the bell of *Dominion of Canada* when it was formally unveiled.

CHAPTER 15

Mallard 75 by royal appointment

N ONE OTHER than HRH The Prince of Wales was the patron of the Great Gathering, with model-maker Hornby as its headline sponsor. Five days after the first Great Gathering of surviving A4 Pacifics had "half dispersed", the three operational A4s having left to resume their duties, July 22, 2013, saw Prince Charles arrive in style for a private viewing of the world's fastest steam locomotive and its two repatriated sisters at the museum.

By then, the prince had become renowned as an enthusiast and had been a good friend to the heritage sector. He was given the honour of naming new-build £3 million A1 Peppercorn Pacific No. 60163 *Tornado* at York station on February 19, 2009, after it began its main line career. On that occasion, LNER apple green-liveried *Tornado* hauled the Royal Train, with the prince on the footplate!

However, this time round, it would be an earlier type of East Coast Main Line Pacific, no less than a Gresley A4, which would bring the Royal Train carrying the prince straight into the former York North shed. And the day would be different to any that had gone before. Because less than six-and-a-half years after No. 4464 *Bittern*, proudly carrying the Prince of Wales' coat of arms, headed his train into the museum's Great Hall at

10am for another reunion with three of its sisters, the prince became a grandfather for the first time.

The visit had been arranged well in advance, and true to his word, the prince kept his engagement. However, at that time, Catherine, Duchess of Cambridge, had already gone into labour and had been admitted to St Mary's Hospital in London earlier that morning. During his visit, aides kept the prince supplied with regular updates of her progress.

Bittern and its Mk.1 support coach had been attached to the Royal Train in the Siemens rail yard at York, and so made only a short journey on this very special of occasions. After *Bittern* moved on to the turntable and brought the train to a standstill, the prince alighted and was greeted by Lord Crathorne, the Lord Lieutenant of North Yorkshire, and other civic dignitaries.

He was then introduced to former *Mallard* driver Bernard Bell, 89, who was once fireman on another locomotive hauling the Royal Train with The Queen on board. "He was very interested in the locomotives and he asked me all sorts of questions about my driving," said Bernard, a former mayor of York. "He seemed very nice."

The prince admitted to Sam Dalby, a pupil at St Wilfrid's RC Primary School, that he had liked trains since he was a boy. Growing up in the final complete decade of steam on the main line, the prince was speaking for a whole generation.

Accompanied by Paul Kirkman in his first official duty since being named museum director on a permanent basis, the prince was taken to *Mallard* and boarded the footplate. He sounded *Mallard's* whistle, powered by an air compressor, to signal for *Bittern* to reverse out of the museum.

He then inspected the two repatriated A4s and was shown the digital video recreation of *Mallard's* 126mph run on Stoke Bank on July 3, 1938, next to the museum's new *Mallard* Simulator where the public could experience the thrills of the record-breaking exploits of 75 years ago.

Afterwards, the prince toured the refurbished Station Hall. He boarded several of the royal carriages including Queen Victoria's favourite carriage, King Edward's saloon and Queen Elizabeth's saloon, used by the royal family during the Second World War. He then unveiled a plaque to mark

Station Hall's official reopening following a major refurbishment.

He left by car for York Minister, where he was greeted by the Archbishop of York, Dr John Sentamu. He was shown the new Revealing York Minster exhibition in the cathedral's undercroft, and even tried his hand at stone-masonry with a hammer and chisel among the craftspeople at the Minster Stoneyard, his next engagements on a two-day tour of Yorkshire.

Back in London, crowds gathered, eagerly awaiting news of the royal birth, which happened at 4.24pm. The Duchess of Cambridge and her baby, accompanied by Prince William, left the hospital the following day. On July 24, the royal baby's name was announced as George Alexander Louis.

CHAPTER 16

Mallard on tour

IN THE weeks that followed the phenomenally-successful first Great Gathering, No. 4468 *Mallard* went on an East Midlands-oriented tour of its own to mark the 75th anniversary of its 126mph world record-breaking run. Despite the fact that it was purely on static display, having not steamed since its 50th anniversary celebrations in 1988, the public response was again astonishing.

The first stop was Grantham station, which stands just north of the Stoke Bank stretch, the legendary East Coast Main Line gradient down which *Mallard's* and many other speed records were both set and broken. *Mallard* had not passed through the Lincolnshire town for more than half a century. However, a special weekend festival at the station was arranged in its honour on September 7-8, 2013. Sponsored by Mortons Media Group, the publisher of *The Railway Magazine*, *Heritage Railway* and *Rail Express*, the event was organised by South Kesteven District Council under the banner of the *Mallard* Grantham Partnership.

The festival ground was based around a siding specially relaid to the immediate south of the main station front, and behind the public car park, by contractor Carillion.

Devon & Cornwall Railways Class 56 No. 56311 towed *Mallard* and one of its ECML successors, Class 55 Deltic No. 55019 *Royal Highland Fusilier*, from York to Grantham, as a small crowd gathered at the city's station to watch the convoy depart on September 4. Entrance to the two-day Story of Speed festival, which also incorporated a host of ancillary events around the town, was free. The event from packed from opening time on the Saturday to closing time on the Sunday, with up to the last minute, lengthy queues of families forming to board *Mallard's* footplate.

From start to finish, people were jostling to have their picture taken in the sunshine with the celebrity engine as a backdrop. Attendance vastly exceeded all expectations, with more than 15,000 turning up over the two days — a figure of which any operational railway gala would have been proud.

On the Saturday evening, a talk entitled The Quest for Speed on Rail took place with Dr Alfred Gottwaldt, senior curator, railways, from the Berlin Technical Museum and Bob Gwynne, the NRM's associate curator of Rail Vehicles, chaired by Nick Pigott, then editor of *The Railway Magazine*, and a native of Grantham. Dr Gottwaldt spoke about the German 'Flying Hamburger' — the ground-breaking two-car diesel railcar set which prompted the LNER and Gresley to show that steam could do better, and which therefore provided an impetus for the design of the streamlined A4s.

On the Sunday, Nick Pigott unveiled a Grantham Civic Society information signboard on Platform 1 beneath the station sign and looking south in the direction of *Mallard's* record-breaking great journey.

Organisers were amazed at the public response to the festival, which prompted talk of a repeat. Spokesman Henry Cleary said: "People have been responding to the beauty of the engine, as well as its history. The town has a wonderful engineering heritage. People are tremendously proud of Sir Nigel Gresley, who designed *Mallard*, and his achievements. What's been fun is that so many locomotive drivers pulling into their station have been sounding their horns as a salute to *Mallard*."

The following Thursday, September 13, *Mallard* was taken back to its Doncaster Works erecting shop birthplace, possibly for the last time ever. There, it broke a banner as it was pushed back out into the daylight in front of 100 ticketed guests and VIPs. That symbolic relaunch preceded a gala dinner in Doncaster's historic Georgian Mansion House attended by dignitaries including Tim Godfrey, grandson of Sir Nigel Gresley.

During the following weekend, September 15-16, *Mallard* was displayed at the Freightliner Ltd Railport in Doncaster, with admission again free. Its appearance deliberately coincided with Doncaster's St Leger Festival Week, echoing the words of world steam speed record-setting driver Joe Duddington. "She couldn't have done better in the St Leger," he said afterwards.

Retired amateur jockey Clare Balding presented Channel 4 coverage of the festival live from *Mallard's* footplate on the Saturday morning. Around 2500 members of the public attended the weekend event at Railport, considerably fewer than the number who turned up at Grantham. Organisers said that this may have been due to the fact that Railport is not immediately accessible from the town centre. FirstGroup laid on shuttle buses for the event to ferry visitors from the station to the Freightliner depot every 10 to 15 minutes, their headboards reading '4468 Mallard.' On the Sunday morning, two of the buses with the special destination boards were lined up alongside the A4.

Anthony Coulls, the NRM's senior curator of railway vehicles, said: "During *Mallard's* big anniversary year we wanted to give the people of Doncaster the chance to see the world's fastest steam locomotive in the town where it was built."

After its appearance at Doncaster, *Mallard* was taken to Chesterfield for the Barrow Hill Live 2013! event which was held at the former Staveley Midland roundhouse on September 28-29. The model-oriented event, sponsored by both Bachmann and Hornby, celebrated 160 years of Doncaster Works by bringing together a range of steam and diesel locomotives that all have an association with the plant. *Mallard* was lined up alongside new-build Peppercorn A1 Pacific No. 60163 *Tornado*, which was celebrating its fifth anniversary of moving for the first time, Following the conclusion of Barrow Hill Live! Class 56 diesel No. 56301 towed *Mallard* back to its York home, where its connecting rods were refitted, in readiness for its appearance in the second line-up of all six surviving A4s at the autumn Great Gathering.

CHAPTER 17

The Autumn Great Gathering and a mystery solved

HOW DO you follow one of the most successful museum events ever held in Britain, just three months later? The first Great Gathering in July 2013 attracted a total attendance of 138,141, including a record-breaking 13,035 on its first Saturday (compared to an average maximum of 3000 for a summer Saturday) making it the most successful in the history of the National Railway Museum since it was opened by HRH The Duke of Edinburgh in September 1975.

Yet would the public appetite be strong enough to justify a second line-up event at the museum in the autumn? The answer was a resounding yes. The Autumn Great Gathering, which began on Saturday, October 26, 2013, and incorporated the school half-term week, was extended to 17 days, due to the owners of the operational trio of A4s not recalling their engines for a further three days than was previously anticipated.

Admission was again free, with visitors being invited to each make a donation at the entrance, while extra charges were made for ticketed events such as early bird photographic sessions, where enthusiasts were able to take pictures of the magnificent six minus the crowds that impaired their vision during normal opening times. Four of the six survivors were shunted into place in the Great Hall of the National Railway Museum in York on Tuesday, October 15. No. 4464 *Bittern*, No. 4468 *Mallard*, No. 4489 *Dominion of Canada* and No. 60008 *Dwight D. Eisenhower* were later joined by No. 60007 *Sir Nigel Gresley* and No. 60009 *Union of South Africa*.

By the end of the first day of the autumn event, nearly 12,000 people had turned up to see the line-up, followed by another 8000 on the Sunday. However, even with the extra days, the attendance did not surpass the number of visitors to the summer event. Yet the total attendance of 108,419 was still hailed as an incredible achievement and a resounding testimony to the enduring appeal of Gresley's streamlined masterpieces.

During the Autumn Great Gathering, museum researchers solved the mystery of the hitherto-unnamed guard who appeared in a photograph of the *Mallard* train crew after the record run. LNER goods guard Henry 'Harry' Croucher was pictured alongside the rest of the train crew in several seminal photographs taken after the run on July 3, 1938.

However, his identity remained a mystery until his daughter Julie Slater from London contacted the museum's associate curator of railway vehicles Bob Gwynne and arranged to visit the event on November 8 with her son Richard Slater from Nottingham. Julie produced family photographs to prove that her dad was on board the train as it raced down Stoke Bank after being drafted in as part of the world steam speed record attempt team, unsuspecting, as were the rest of the crew, of what the true purpose of the 'braking test' trip was. Her late brother Bert also worked for the LNER before he died in a naval battle while serving during the Second World War.

Bob said: "Our Mallard 75 celebrations have given us a new strand in the *Mallard* story. There is absolutely no doubt that the man in the family photos Julie provided is the same man as in the picture taken of the record-breaking crew at Peterborough. Harry would have been quite pleased at being asked to work on that Sunday's 'brake trial' as it would have meant double time, but of all the crew in the picture he looks like he found it quite a hair-raising experience.

"Unfortunately he had already died before our 50th anniversary celebrations, so it has taken the added publicity surrounding the 75th anniversary to encourage Julie and her family to step forward and talk about their strong connection to our celebrity locomotive."

In the Great Hall, Julie said: "I feel overwhelmed that I'm here. Now I can let everyone know who my father was."

MEN WHO MADE THE A4S 'HAPPEN'

There is no doubting the magnificence of the LNER A4 streamlined Pacifics and the brilliance of their design. However, the performance of any locomotive can only be as good as the men on the footplate. While plans to borrow the two A4s from their North American museum homes were being drawn up, the National Railway Museum's associate curator of rail vehicles Bob Gwynne suggested staging the biggest reunion of A4 fireman and drivers held in the heritage era — and no stone was left unturned in attempts by museum researchers to track down the surviving locomen, many by then in their eighties and nineties.

More than 90 were contacted, and on October 26, 2013, the first day of the autumn Great Gathering, around 80 footplate veterans were assembled at the museum, many meeting for the first time since the end of steam, exchanging old drivers' tales and reminiscences. Several of them brought diaries of their days on the footplate and shovel, proudly kept since.

Indeed, so many former drivers and firemen turned up for the event that they had to be divided into two rooms, one for those from King's Cross 'Top Shed' and another for those who were based at other major East Coast Main Line sheds, including Edinburgh Haymarket, York, Doncaster, Gateshead, Peterborough, Carlisle, and Newton Heath.

One of these guests was 88-year-old Walter Blazey. A regular fireman on *Dwight D. Eisenhower* for two years, he began work as a cleaner at 'Top Shed' in 1941. His first job was to clean another Gresley masterpiece — the experimental W1 No. 10000 'Hush-Hush', the only 4-6-4 tender locomotive to run in Britain. It had hit a bullock the day before, and the remains had to be cleaned off. He then spent 13 years as a fireman on A4s, before working as a driver for 25 years. In total, he spent 48 years in service at the legendary King's Cross shed.

Walter broke his arm when he was a fireman on an A4 by catching it on the water scoop handle on the tender as he took on water at speed at Balby, south of Doncaster. In the 1950s, he recalled taking *Bittern* past Essendine — a stone's throw from Little Bytham, the scene of *Mallard's* world speed record — at 117mph.

Like many of his fellow East Coast Main Line drivers of the day, when dieselisation came, Walter went on to drive Class 55 Deltic diesels. He fondly recalled an occasion where, on a King's Cross to Doncaster turn in 1959, he brought the Royal Train down to 18mph at Potters Bar so sharply that everyone in the sleeping cars including the Duke of Edinburgh fell out of bed. "Prince Philip walked straight past me," he recalled.

Sam Jenkins, the traction inspector — the same who had been on the footplate of *Mallard* as it reached 126mph on July 3, 1938, told him sharply to report to his office the next morning. After entering with some trepidation, Walter was told that the sudden braking was not his fault, and instead had been traced back to a valve that had not worked correctly.

Alfred Smith, 92, recalled *Mallard* ascending Stoke Bank at 90mph during speed trials in 1952, with King's Cross shedmaster Peter Townend on board. Suddenly, the connecting road snapped, "and Peter Townend was out of the corridor tender as fast as anyone could move," he recalled. King's Cross driver Rob Birch, who started on the railways in 1947 at the age of 14, recalled an incident when he was on the footplate of *Mallard* with the 9.20am from King's Cross when, after passing the water troughs at Newark, a lump of coal flew through a window of a house near a level crossing. Police were called over fears that someone could have been injured.

Former Doncaster locoman George Purnell, who also attended the reunion, had worked as a fireman to driver Tommy Bray, the fireman on *Mallard's* record-breaking run. He described travelling at speed on an A4 as 'exhilarating.' George said that he left the railway in 1954 after realising he would never become a driver before steam was phased out... and had no intention of driving diesels. Special pride of place went to Maurice Dakin, who worked on all six surviving A4s during their British Railways days. "I fired most of the A4s that were at King's Cross," he said. "I enjoyed it all so much — they were all good memories."

Before the Great Gatherings were staged, there had been criticism of the cost of temporarily repatriating *Dwight D. Eisenhower* and *Dominion of Canada* for the event. The repatriation was heavily sponsored, but the museum later disclosed that the cost would be £231,000. Should we be spending that sort of taxpayers' money in a recession, and depleting the reserves of the Science Museum Group, the question was asked.

However, those who visited one or both events had another question to ask. After standing for hours in queues at the museum's three catering outlets to get served and seeing mountains of souvenirs in the retail outlets quickly denuded, everyone began asking – how much money are they making?

Confounding the initial critics, once the museum had done its sums, it was found that even before the Great Goodbye was held at the Locomotion museum in Shildon, a total of £404,500 'profit' had been made – to be reinvested in the Science Museum group. The figures were broken down as follows:

Firstly, the NRM received cash sponsorship and donations towards the Mallard 75 celebrations of £242,271 which more than covered the specific costs of bringing *Dominion of Canada* and *Dwight D. Eisenhower* home and safely returning them at the end of the two-year loan period. The transcontinental move was brought within the Science Museum's financial grasp only thanks to the received £260,000 and promised £240,000 of in-kind support from the museum's project partners including haulage company Moveright International, shipping company ACL, Peel Ports in the UK plus Ceres and Canadian National Railways in Canada.

The Science Museum Group provided just over £231,000 in capital support to the overall Mallard 75 project which in addition to the repatriation costs, an identical figure, also included all aspects of the display of the 'big six'. That ranged from the ceremonial shunt of *Mallard* on July 3 in front of the world media to more mundane expenses such as specially designed stairs for footplate access – a big winner with the public at both York events – essential asbestos remediation work and insurance.

The £231,000 repatriation and return figure was a projected cost based on actual and estimated expenditure by the museum and its project partners, and not only covered insurance, asbestos remediation, hire costs and rail movements, but also includes a sizeable contingency fund for any problems arising in regard to the return journey.

Although a drop in the ocean in museum redevelopment terms — by comparison, the British Museum's extension to house its then-new world conservation and exhibitions centre cost £135 million — the figure nonetheless comprised a sizeable investment in today's cash-strapped environment. The commercial turnover for the first two Great Gatherings was more than £1 million, providing a return to the Science Museum Group of nearly £497,000 — a tremendous return on investment for a not-for-profit organisation whose measure for success is the volume of people it educates and informs about science and engineering.

During the events, visitors gave a total of just under £140,000 in donations at the door, plus gift aid. The museum brought in a further £50,000 with its ticketed photography and dining events.

During the first Great Gathering, the Friends of the National Railway Museum took £76,000, the profit from which should have more than covered the group's donation of £50,000 towards the cosmetic restoration of the two North American A4s. Furthermore, *Mallard's* September appearances at Grantham, Doncaster and Barrow Hill, as described in the previous chapter, earned £6000 in loan fees.

The commercial statistics were more than impressive. In early 2014, the total cash sponsorship and donations for the Mallard 75 project were said to be £242,300. While the total forecast cost was given as £530,700, once income from nearly a quarter of a million visitors had been taken into account, £404,500 was left over to be invested in the work of the Science Museum Group.

A museum spokesman said: "The National Railway Museum, like all national museums, is a not-for-profit organisation and its specific mission is to enable people to have a life-enhancing experience through exploring the story of railways. 'Big wow' events like the Great Gatherings are perhaps among the few ways museums can attract repeat visits and pull in new visitors in these times of austerity when a day out for the family has to be carefully considered.

"Ask any one of those visitors in July and October if they found it a life-enhancing experience and I am sure they will answer in the affirmative. Although it was a major undertaking to bring two Doncaster-built locomotives home to the UK for a two-year visit, the resulting news splash got people talking about *Mallard* and the anniversary. The bold scheme to bring together all six surviving members of the A4 class and the engineering ingenuity required to extract the borrowed locos and transport them home also fitted perfectly with the overall mission of the Science Museum Group, which is to engage people in a dialogue about the history, present and future of human ingenuity in the fields of science, technology, medicine, transport and media.

"The Great Gathering events also fitted in with the essence of the NRM which is to connect generations through the wonderful stories of railways and how they shape our world."

Figures showed that museum visitor numbers by January 2014 had soared by 35% on the figure for previous year. At its autumn annual conference, local tourism organisation Visit York praised Mallard 75 for the best visitor numbers to the city in decades. During the Autumn Great Gathering, the six A4s were showcased in a way that even Sir Nigel Gresley would never have envisaged, for the hugely-successful event encompassed the fifth annual Locos In a Different Light competition.

This contest, staged as part of the wider Illuminating York festival, saw the line-up of six A4s bathed in theatrical lighting and artificial smoke effects by teams of students from all over Britain.

Theatricality, energy consumption, conservation and safety, not necessarily the most striking exhibit, were the criteria by which the teams were judged by industry professionals at a VIP preview evening on October 29. The newly-opened Da Vinci Studio School of Creative Enterprise in Letchworth, Hertfordshire, whose students illuminated *Dominion of Canada* in fluorescent lighting which reflected that nation's flag, was the winner.

Over and above the bumper daytime attendances, Locos In a Different Light attracted 10,399 visitors — a figure which compares very favourably with a well-attended gala at a top heritage railway over the same period.

CHAPTER 18

The 21st century A4 speed king: Bittern hits 94mph

I**N PARALLEL** with the Mallard 75 events, special dispensation was given to one of the six surviving A4s to run three public trips at 90mph on the East Coast Main Line. That locomotive was No. 4464 *Bittern*, and the trips were organised by owner Jeremy Hosking's Locomotive Services Limited in conjunction with Pathfinder Tours, backed by Network Rail engineers and Vehicle Acceptance Board inspectors.

The green light for the specials was given by Network Rail following the successful completion of high-speed trials when *Bittern*, hauling eight coaches, achieved 90mph on former Western Region metals between Didcot and Reading, as described in Chapter 13.

The first of the three specials, the 'Ebor Streak', ran to schedule on June 29 – setting a new heritage era official speed record of 92.5mph.However, the following two high-speed runs, the 'Tyne-Tees Streak' and the 'Capital Streak', were cancelled due to Network Rail's summer fire risk steam ban. Originally dated for July 19 and then rearranged in the first instance for August 30, the 'Tyne-Tees Streak' eventually ran on Thursday, December 5.

Departing Bristol Temple Meads for York behind DB Schenker Class

67 No. 67006, the 'Tyne-Tees Streak' set out for York with 10 full coaches. It was a day when the run-Pathfinder's train was again threatened by adverse weather conditions which had reduced all service train speeds working north of York to a maximum of 50mph because of storm force winds, strong enough to rock the station's footbridge

However, Network Rail came up trumps. Rather than postpone the train again because of the weather and the real risk of tree branches falling on to the wires, it was allowed to proceed. The decision could not prevent the 'Tyne-Tees Streak' departing for Newcastle an hour late, partly due to the late running of a southbound train bringing *Bittern's* driver to start his shift.

Passengers were certainly not disappointed by the performance of the A4, which worked the train from York to Newcastle and back. The outward journey was affected by gales that severely depleted normal services and accordingly the train had to run at restricted speed. The wind died down somewhat for the return leg, which was ambitiously scheduled to take 67 minutes for the 80.2 miles to York at an average timetabled speed of 71.8mph.

Maximum permissible speed derogations had been granted, easing the normal 75mph to 90mph for long stretches. Apart from slowing to 75mph for a bridge restriction at Northallerton, driver Steve Hanszar, fireman Keith Mufin and traction inspector Bob Hart combined to work the A4 up to 90mph for long periods. There have been very few steam-hauled start-to-stop runs from Newcastle-York. The fastest was recorded in LNER days, in the form of a 1946 trial run with A4 No. 2512 *Silver Fox* on six coaches, taking 68 minutes four seconds.

With 10 coaches grossing around 370 tonnes, *Bittern* beat that record by 66 seconds by taking 66 minutes 58 seconds, according to *The Railway Magazine's* practice and performance expert John Heaton, who was on board. In the magazine's January 2014 issue, John wrote: "Some recorders have claimed the run to be another 38 seconds faster. There had been a hesitant start and possibly momentary halt, from which point some recorders adjusted their timings. If the train did indeed stop, and many at the rear of the train are doubtful, no doors were released and it was not subject to a second 'right-away', so it was in fact no different from any other form of delay en route."

Accelerating away from the permanent 85mph speed restriction at Aycliffe, speed crept towards the magic 90mph and hit 94mph on the 1-in-220 downgrade to Parkgate Junction. Passengers spontaneously applauded as the speed peaked. The Thirsk to Tollerton leg showed an average of 91.2mph with a maximum of 92mph.

Locomotive Services Limited's general manager Richard Corser afterwards told *Heritage Railway* that the speed had peaked at 93mph.

Passenger John Turner, who was seated in the front coach, told the magazine that he and others all witnessed 95mph displayed on a tablet with a GPS speedometer app and photographed the screen for posterity. It must here be pointed out, however, that GPS devices have been challenged as to their accuracy. The highlight of the run was on *Mallard's* 1938 racing ground. John Heaton said: "After passing Grantham at 76.6mph, speed dropped to no lower than 71.16mph on the climb to Stoke summit, this time with 11 coaches and around 405 tonnes gross. After a compulsory slowing at Little Bytham, *Bittern* then took the 9.2 miles from Essendine to Werrington Junction at a flying average of 91.2mph with a maximum speed of 92mph."

John said: "It was a brilliant ride back from Newcastle to York and more than made up for the rather sedate 50mph limit demanded for the journey north earlier in the day."

MALLARD'S RACETRACK REVISITED

The 'Capital Streak', originally booked to run on July 27 and moved to August 31, finally ran on Saturday, December 7. *Bittern* hauled the train from York to King's Cross with water stops at Retford and Conington South, and was again in sparkling form, running consistently at 90mph. The weather on the day was very different to that of the previous Thursday, as high winds had dropped and southbound services from York were back to normal.

With drivers Steve Hanszar and Mark Dale, fireman Dave Proctor and traction inspectors Gareth Jones and Colin Kerswill taking turns on the footplate, *Bittern* departed from York at 2.19pm with 11 full coaches behind the drawbar. The A4 quickly accelerated to its normal line speed and then topped the 90mph mark after Doncaster racing towards Retford and Newark — where the 'Ebor Streak' was clocked at 92.5mph in June.

Of course, the highlight of the trips was the run over the section of track where *Mallard* achieved its 126mph, and which is now marked by a trackside sign. John Heaton said: "After passing Grantham at 76½mph, speed dropped to no lower than 71½mph on the climb to Stoke summit, this time with 11 coaches and around 405 tonnes gross. After a compulsory slowing at Little Bytham, *Bittern* then took the 9.2 miles from Essendine to Werrington Junction at a flying average of 91.2mph with a maximum speed of 92mph."

Approaching the home straight, the 'Capital Streak' run was curtailed when a double yellow at Huntingdon and a 'feather' indicated that the train was being turned on to the Down slow line to let late running service trains pass.

Baulked by signals and slow line running, the train was reported arriving at King's Cross 36 minutes late — but did it matter? *Bittern's* mission had been accomplished in style. It could be described only as a pulsating tribute to Sir Nigel Gresley's fleet of A4s. However, it was not about breaking records. The two 90mph trains were about showing that ageing but well-maintained steam locomotives are capable of holding their own on Britain's 21st-century national network. For *Bittern* and two sister A4s, there would be more to come before the last of the three Great Gatherings.

When Steve Davies and his team reached agreement to borrow the two A4s from North America, it was on the understanding that the pair would not be displayed at other venues. However, once they were over in Britain, Barrow Hill roundhouse, which had built up a solid track record of classic events including line-ups of LNER locomotives even though it is deep within LMS territory, was granted special dispensation by the US National Railroad Museum and Exporail to borrow No. 4489 *Dominion of Canada* and No. 60008 *Dwight D. Eisenhower* for a one-off event.

Titled East Coast Giants, more than 6000 people turned up over the weekend of February 8-9, 2014, for the big appeal of Barrow Hill, as far as the expatriate A4s was concerned, was that it presented the only chance to view and photograph the locomotives in a classic working engine shed and rail yard setting, as opposed to a museum venue.

The pair were lined up alongside A2 No. 60532 *Blue Peter* in the Roundhouse yard, with No. 4464 *Bittern*, which hauled passenger trains up the venue's Springwell branch, making regular appearances in the line-up. Meanwhile, new-build Peppercorn A1 Pacific No. 60163 *Tornado*, undergoing planned annual maintenance at the Roundhouse, attracted much attention in its prime position on the turntable.

CHAPTER 19

The Great Goodbye

S HILDON IN County Durham owes its existence to railways. Already a centre of the booming local coal mining industry of the 18th and early 19th centuries which was served by a network of horse-drawn wagonways, it was there in 1825 that the Stockton & Darlington Railway opened its workshops. On September 27 that year, the first public passenger train ran over what was the world's first steam-operated public railway, and at the time of writing there were major celebrations planned to mark its bicentenary in 2025.

Many of the early pioneer steam locomotives such as Timothy Hackworth's *Sans Pareil* were built at the workshops. The railway owned much of the surrounding land and little Shildon mushroomed in size to having a population of around 9000. Indeed, it is with total justification that the town became known as the 'cradle of the railways'.

After the Second World War, Shildon had one of the biggest sidings complexes in Europe and was established as a major centre for wagon building. However, in 1984 the wagon works closed, ending a proud legacy that had begun in the days of George and Robert Stephenson. Nine years earlier, a major cavalcade of historic locomotives and modern traction led by a replica of the Stockton & Darlington *Locomotion No. 1* was held on

August 31, 1975, to mark the 150th anniversary of the Stockton & Darlington Railway. That was the same year in which the National Railway Museum at York was opened, combining the earlier York Railway Museum and the British Transport Museum at Clapham.

In 2004, a purpose-designed branch of the NRM was opened alongside the route of the Stockton & Darlington Railway at Shildon by local MP and then Prime Minister Tony Blair, affording valuable under cover storage to National Collection vehicles for which there was no space at York. Its extensive site includes the former Timothy Hackworth Museum, which contains the original *Sans Pareil*, and the inventor's home.

Named Locomotion: The National Railway Museum at Shildon, it was designed to accommodate 60,000 visitors a year. As is the case at the NRM in York, under government policy admission is free. From the start, the museum was more successful than anyone had dared hope, as visitor numbers exceeded original estimates. However, a new all-time high was reached during the February 15-23, 2014, the school half-term week, when thanks to its impeccable railway pedigree all eyes were once again focused on Shildon.

Public steam railways began with the likes of *Sans Pareil* and Stephenson's *Rocket*, but in many ways reached a summit when *Mallard* set an all-time world steam speed record well over a century later. It was therefore appropriate that the last of the three Mallard 75 Great Gatherings was staged at Locomotion.

A hoped-for 60,000 visitors a year? That figure was passed at the Great Goodbye during the first five days of the nine-day event — by the end of which a total of 119,880 visitors had passed through the doors to pay homage to the unique outdoor line-ups of British transport technology's art deco finest. By contrast, the museum's previous best visitor attendance for an event was recorded in 2010, when new-build A1 Peppercorn Pacific No. 60163 *Tornado* was displayed for four days. That event attracted 21,000 visitors.

In February 2014, however, sleepy Shildon was yanked back into life. If anyone had forgotten about its rich railway past, they were reminded with a jolt. On roads approaching the Locomotion museum's car parks, tailbacks of traffic well over a mile long built up as crowds flocked in the February sunshine to see the A4s, climb on to their footplates, or take a brakevan ride behind one of the legendary giants of steam.

Northern Rail, which runs services on the Darlington to Bishop Auckland branch, part of the original Stockton & Darlington Railway, introduced extra trains for the duration of the Great Goodbye, upping the frequency from two hourly to one, and doubling them in size from two-car Class 142 diesel multiple sets to twin-set rakes. Still it was barely enough, as many of the trains were packed to standing room only.

Locomotion officials had 'guesstimated' an attendance of around 70,000 for the week. By the second day, it was clear that this figure was way wide of the mark. By the Sunday, lengthy queues of visitors tailed back from the entrance as staff were forced to limit the number of admissions due to fire regulations. However, those waiting in the queue for an hour or more still had a grandstand view not only of the A4s but also of No. 4464 *Bittern* hauling short brakevan rides along the museum's internal running line.

Trade boomed in the town throughout the event. One pub reported a boost in takings of 300%. Another which normally served 100 meals a week saw the figure rise to more than 250. For the day's events, the six A4s were not lined up evenly as had been the case at York. Five of them were arranged on the museum yard apron in a staggered formation, in order to place large wooden steps alongside them to allow cab access to visitors.

From the moment the doors opened at 9.30am each day to closing time at 5pm, endless queues of people wanting to 'cab' an A4 formed alongside each of the five. Each day, one of the three operative A4s would offer brakevan trips from the museum platform, so did not form part of the line-up on the apron. However, a series of midweek evening enthusiast photographic charters at £90-a-head were held, at which all six A4s were lined up together on the museum's apron. Solihull-based Martin Creese of 30742 Charters was brought in by Locomotion to organise the events, which were quickly sold out.

The rain which had caused extensive flooding in many parts of England during the preceding weeks luckily held off and the bumper attendances showed no sign of abating. On the final Saturday, more than 18,000 visitors turned up. One of the big highlights of the Great Goodbye was the public Mallard 75 gala dinner which was held at Locomotion on the evening of Friday, February 21. Introduced by then NRM head Paul Kirkman, who oversaw the Mallard 75 year of celebrations, the guest speaker was none other than the man who dreamed up the whole affair — his predecessor Steve Davies.

Steve said: "What we have witnessed has been remarkable from whichever angle you view it. Visitor number records have been blown out of the water; significant retail and commercial revenue streams have given a major financial shot in the arm to the York and Shildon operations, and to the Science Museum Group as a whole; the national and international press have lavished the NRM with unprecedented levels of positive coverage; royal and High Commissioner-level patronage has provided a rich coating of gloss and gravitas to events; the world's enthusiasts have flocked to the NRM's door, the most distant from a South Pacific island; and most importantly the event has been fun.

"But why did we do it? What possible reason could there be for a nation to go all dewy-eyed about six large lumps of metal with pointy fronts, as a non-enthusiast friend of mine put it? How could the mere act of gathering together the last six lucky survivors of the most aesthetically pleasing class of steam locomotive ever built create such a riot of enthusiasm and delight? Well the reasons are not hard to find if you possess an understanding of the psyche of the British people.

"We are a race which loves our railways. We love to complain about them too — but we love them all the same. We like nothing better than to enjoy a jolly good commemoration, preferably really historic, and if it is to celebrate something that we as a nation are immensely proud of, so much the better. Mallard's record breaking anniversary therefore had to be celebrated. But the 75th birthday called for something seriously imaginative, particularly as there was no prospect of the locomotive being returned to traffic for the event.

"At a time of national austerity, perhaps the country needed a lift; to be reminded of its considerable engineering achievements. Perhaps our contemporary modern railway network needed a celebratory event around which it could fully unite with the railway heritage movement. Or then again, was it a time for the National Railway Museum to demonstrate its world-leading status, and to employ its corporate and reputational muscle to make something very special happen? These and many other motives were present to varying degrees throughout the project.

"But whatever the motives, this has nevertheless been a project which fundamentally flew on the back of an innate gut instinct that the sheer audacity of assembling all six surviving A4s would capture the public imagination. There was no market-tested analysis involved; no focus groups proposing risk-free but bland compromise solutions; no business case looking at the commercial viability of such an operation; and certainly no fall-back plan in the event that sponsorship was not forthcoming.

"No, this was a project that depended for success on a compellingly articulated vision which potential sponsors and supporters alike would feel instinctively drawn to. A vision that the overseas organisations involved would feel they did not wish to miss out on. A vision which was clear that this seminal anniversary should become a vehicle to reach out to the overwhelmingly non-enthusiast majority of this country. And a vision that would be driven through to successful completion regardless of the challenges and its detractors.

"The fact that two of the locomotives involved were on the other side of the Atlantic simply added to the project's attractive complexity. Who will ever forget the sense of escalating dramatic expectation as the locomotives concerned undertook their complex journey from foreign shores back to their country of birth? We were all frustratingly hungry for information, rather like an expectant father being ordered to sit in the waiting room during the delivery of his first-born. Let's be clear – it was the transatlantic dimension that made Mallard 75 the success that it has become. If all six locomotives had been based in the UK, then the 'mission impossible' nature of Mallard 75 would have been seriously diluted.

"Future reunions would always have been viewed as a possibility, so it was this never-to-be-repeated aspect of the project which was eventually to become the main reason for its success. Although much focus has been on *Dwight D. Eisenhower* and *Dominion of Canada*; paradoxically the most important first step in organising Mallard 75 was not to approach our opposite numbers in Green Bay and Montreal, but to write confidentially to the private owners of *Sir Nigel Gresley, Union of South Africa* and *Bittern* outlining the plan, swearing them to secrecy, and asking for their agreement to take part. For if only one of them had declined then the whole point of the exercise would have been defeated and it would have been pointless even discussing the matter with our North American allies.

"I am delighted to report that they all replied in the affirmative by return of post, and kept the project a closely-guarded secret despite the many discussions and meetings we held to pull the programme together. *Mallard's* participation as a nationally owned asset was a given, but I think we should be collectively grateful that the private owners of the UK-based A4s so readily took part in the celebrations with what must have been an impact on their respective income streams. They shared the vision and helped make it a reality, and I believe we should now show our appreciation in time-honoured fashion.

"Ambitious plans need a sprinkling of heroes to make them happen. This story is no different. It was heroic of the National Railroad Museum, Green Bay, and Exporail, the Canadian Railway Museum in Montreal, to entrust their precious locomotives to the care of the National Railway Museum in the first place. Their response to my initial phone call was cautiously positive, but they subsequently very enthusiastically hosted the many technical visits which were necessary to get this complex project off the ground. Both museums were quick to grasp the potential benefits for their respective international profiles of joining us in this venture and I hope they feel that they have reaped a significant reward in this respect.

"The Friends of the National Railway Museum were equally heroic in trusting their instincts and investing in the cosmetic restoration of our transatlantic visitors. The promise to cosmetically restore the locomotives on arrival in the UK was a key incentive in negotiating the loans, and I breathed a huge sigh of relief when the Friends Council agreed the £50,000 needed. I gather, though, that their investment has been turned into a healthy profit in retail sales. The actual restoration of the locomotives was heroic too, and much praise should be heaped in particular on the now-famous 'blue team' here at Shildon whose work to convert *Dominion of Canada* to 1937 fully-valanced condition complete with single chimney, chrome fittings, Canadian Pacific Bell and chime whistle must rate as one of the more eye-catching aspects of the overall project.

"Our many sponsors and supporters pulled together magnificently, but special mention must go to Atlantic Container Line. They really were central to all this, and their calm and reassuring attitude when we missed the first planned sailing out of Halifax was just what was needed at a very stressful moment.

"Mallard 75 went way beyond the physical confines of York and Shildon, and we should also recognise the inspired combined efforts of Network Rail, East Coast, Northern Rail, West Coast Railways, DB Schenker and many other main line operators, and of course *Bittern's* owners, for not only facilitating a remarkable series of high-speed A4 runs but also for enabling the movement on network tracks of a significant number of steam and diesel locomotives in a Mallard 75 context.

"The biggest heroes by far were Andrew Goodman and his lads from Moveright International. It is no exaggeration to say that without him and his team none of this would have happened. I invited Andrew in for a chat as the idea was brewing in my mind to discuss the challenges of moving locomotives across the Atlantic, and this quickly led to him volunteering his skills and expertise. When I first saw *Dwight D. Eisenhower* hermetically sealed into its museum building in Green Bay, I was convinced the project would founder. He convinced me otherwise.

"Andrew and his team put in huge amounts of planning time while still running his day-to-day business. They were subsequently out of the country for over two months, dealing tenaciously with every problem and issue that such a complex move could throw at them, keeping their cool, summoning every ounce of initiative, and doing their utmost to ensure that an excited and expectant British population was not disappointed.

"The Monster Moves programme was quite breath-taking in its portrayal of a man utterly determined to achieve the impossible on behalf of his country. Andrew, I and many others owe you a deep debt of gratitude. You are the star of this particular show.

"Pessimistic as it may seem, I personally seriously doubt that all six A4s will be assembled in one place again. *Dwight D. Eisenhower* and *Dominion of Canada* will soon return to their native shores and to a spectacular welcome home. They have acted as important ambassadors for their respective owning museums and will be taking pride of place in refreshed gallery spaces where their story can be told to great effect. There will simply be no incentive for them to pay a return visit to the UK for a very long time, if ever. That, I'm afraid, is it.

"So let us be eternally grateful that Mallard 75 happened in our lifetimes and that so many people and organisations came together to make it happen. We should now use its powerful legacy to maintain the interest and enthusiasm of the many converts it achieved to the modern and heritage railway cause. I look forward to seeing you all at the Mallard 100 event in 2038 when I will be 79 years old!"

The next day, fans gathered at Locomotion to watch the start of the third and final break-up of the Great Gathering. *Union of South Africa* coupled up to *Mallard* before towing it via the East Coast Main Line to its permanent home at York, its anniversary celebrations finally over. With *Sir Nigel Gresley* leaving the following day and *Bittern* the day after that, the repatriated pair were left on their own. Visitors to Locomotion were still able to see them until Easter, after which they began their return transatlantic voyage from Liverpool, the reverse of their outward journey as described in Chapter 11. Again, the man masterminding the return trip was Andrew Goodman.

After being unloaded at Halifax in Nova Scotia, they were transported on the back of flat cars to No. 4489's home, the Exporail museum in Montreal. There, the pair were posed for one last picture before being split apart again, possibly for the last time ever, with *Dwight D. Eisenhower* returning to its home in Green Bay and bringing the last vestiges of the Great Gathering to a final close.

MALLARD THE MAN!

Driver Percy Elcoat worked for the LNER's main rival, the LMS, in 1951. Yet he was so enamoured of *Mallard* that he decided to name his son after the world record breaker.

Percy told his wife Ethel that when they had a child, he wanted to name the baby after the 'Streak'. Ethel was not overly impressed, but gave in provided he had the more usual David as a middle name.

However, when he was tired of being the butt of duck jokes at school and as a teenager, young Mallard switched his names around to David Mallard Elcoat and it has stayed that way ever since. Aged 63, on Monday, February 18, 2014 he was united with his mechanical namesake at Locomotion during the Great Goodbye and brought his birth certificate along.

He said: "I am extremely proud of my unusual name which always received a lot of interest. However, in my late teens I was getting quite a bit of banter about it and that's when I decided to adopt the use of David — my mother wasn't very happy about this. My wife also frequently reminds me that I should be proud of my birth name. I am a coach driver and over more recent years I have started to tell people about the story of my name when I take them round — and they are always keen to listen.

"I am so pleased that I am able to be part of the event and come to the museum to see the A4s; not surprisingly I am a bit of a rail enthusiast myself and it was an amazing opportunity for myself and many others. I was proud to stand next to *Mallard* at the museum."

Sarah Towers, marketing communications officer at Locomotion, said: "So many people feel a personal connection with the locomotives and this is another interesting story linked to the A4s."

CHAPTER 20

The ultimate steam legend?

IN THE years following the Great Goodbye, controversy flared after the Gresley Society commissioned artist Hazel Reeves to sculpt a £95,000 7ft 4in bronze statue of Sir Nigel Gresley – to be erected on the western concourse on King's Cross station.

Her original design, which received wide support, had a duck standing next to the great chief mechanical engineer, recalling *Mallard's* immortal exploit on Stoke Bank in 1937. However, Gresley's grandsons Ben and the late Tim Godfrey, objected to the inclusion of the duck, saying it was demeaning to his memory.

The society's trust board accordingly decided to discard the duck from the statue. Instead, as a nod to the world record, the statue holds a magazine with 'Mallard' as its cover headline. The decision to remove the duck sparked resignations by trust officials who had been instrumental in commissioning the statue. Society vice chairman Philip Benham denied that the decision to remove the duck was made purely according to the wishes of the grandsons, and said several other factors had been taken into account.

However, more than 3300 people signed a petition calling for the duck to be reinstated, claiming it would spark wider public interest in Gresley's achievements, especially amongst the young, but to no avail. The duck would not appear.

Hazel said: "Sir Nigel Gresley designed steam engines that pushed boundaries of both speed and elegance of design. I hope that my statue of this great engineer helps ensure his achievements are rediscovered and celebrated for generations to come."

In front of a crowd of around 200, the duck-less statue was unveiled by Network Rail chairman Sir Peter Hendy on April 5, 2016, on the 75th anniversary of Gresley's death. Sir Peter said: "This marvellous sculpture commemorates a man who looked relentlessly forward in his day to more powerful locomotives, faster locomotives and the world steam speed record with *Mallard*. We're proud to have Sir Nigel on our station as a commemoration to a great railway mechanical engineer who pushed the technical boundaries of the steam locomotive further than anyone else."

For the occasion, the society's Gresley GNR N2 0-6-2T No. 1744 was parked in Platform 8, coupled to the Severn Valley Railway Charitable Trust's Gresley-designed kitchen composite carriage No. 7960. In the aftermath of the statue's unveiling, press reports stated that small yellow plastic ducks had been positioned on the statue, and the pictures posted afterwards on social media.

In 2021, moves were set in motion in Doncaster to honour one of its greatest sons, Joe Duddington, who drove *Mallard* to the world steam speed record, by restoring the unmarked grave in Hyde Park Cemetery where he was buried in 1953, alongside his wife Mary Alice who died in 1921.

The Friends of Hyde Park Cemetery launched an appeal to give Joe the resting place he deserves in recognition of his achievement and his importance in the railway history of both the town and the UK. Backed by the local *Doncaster Free Press*, the Friends group asked for £2000 to pay for a headstone. The appeal target was smashed twice within a week, raising £5000. The dark grey headstone was ordered from India and the extra money would be used to add kerbing and decorative stones – plus an interpretation panel to explain the circumstances of the world-beating run down Stoke Bank. Matt Delaney, Joe's great-grandson, told the *Doncaster Free Press*: "We have always been proud of him, and it brings a tear to my eye to see *Mallard*, and to have sat where he sat on the footplate. For me, it's a very emotional thing. All I have is stories from my grandmother. The story was that for him, it was just a day at the office — driving trains was his job. When I was at school, if ever asked if there was something interesting about myself I could tell the others, it was that my great-granddad was a train driver and is in the Guinness Book of Records. People had heard of *Mallard*. But he was the driver. Everyone knows of Donald Campbell and Bluebird. It should be the same with Joseph Duddington and *Mallard*. I felt he should have some sort of recognition."

At the time of writing, the National Railway Museum has no plans to restore *Mallard* to running order in the foreseeable future, and it will continue to take pride of place in the Great Hall at York. Neither of the North American museum owners of *Dwight D. Eisenhower* and *Dominion of Canada* have indicated that they intend to do anything with them apart from leave them on permanent static display.

So what about the other three survivors? John Cameron, owner of No. 60009 *Union of South Africa*, has indicated that after its extended boiler ticket expires in 2002, he intends to place it on permanent static display on a visitor centre that he intends to build in Fife, but his first attempt at gaining planning permission for it was refused.

The boiler certificate of No. 60007 *Sir Nigel Gresley* expired in September 2015, and it moved to the National Railway Museum for its overhaul to be carried out in public view in its York workshops. The overhaul was then delayed due to the museum's closure during the COVID-19 pandemic.

In 2019, the Sir Nigel Gresley Locomotive Trust Ltd announced that it had agreed a partnership with Jeremy Hosking's Royal Scot Locomotive & General Trust for No. 60007 to be based at the latter's Crewe depot for main line tours as well as visiting heritage railways including the North Yorkshire Moors Railway, where it is intended to retain strong links. No. 60007 will be operated primarily by Locomotive Services (TOC) Ltd and will haul Saphos Trains' railtours along with the company's existing fleet of locomotives, but will also be available to other operators.

The main line certificate of Jeremy's own A4, No. 4464 *Bittern*, expired in January 2015, after which it ran on the Mid-Hants Railway prior to being withdrawn from service for a major overhaul Crewe. It June 2018 it was moved to Jeremy's Locomotive Storage Ltd facility set up in the iconic former Hornby Hobbies building in Margate's Westwood retail park, where it will remain until its turn to be overhauled at Crewe comes.

Jeremy, who owns 25 locomotives, is developing a major railway museum, the One:One Collection at the site, which was sold to Locomotive Storage for £2.25 million in 2017. London-based Haptic Architects subsequently won a competition to design the museum to be located inside the 12,000 square metre warehouse currently being used to store rolling stock, including *Bittern*. Thanet MPs Sir Roger Gale and Craig Mackinlay indicated support for the project. The adjacent building in Ramsgate Road houses the Hornby Visitor Centre, with Hornby Hobbies now a tenant of Locomotive Storage.

Another dimension of the history of the A4s was brought sharply into focus on the site in 2021, with the unveiling of the end result of a major project to return LNER Beavertail observation car No.1729 to 1937 as-built condition. No. 1729 is one of two distinctive observation cars built for the LNER's King's Cross to Edinburgh Waverley streamlined two-tone-blue-liv-eried crack luxury express passenger train 'The Coronation', named to mark the accession of King George VI and inaugurated on July 5, 1937. The Beavertails were designed by Gresley using similar aerodynamic principles to his A4 Pacifics.

'The Coronation' ceased to run after the outbreak of the Second World War; its coaches were stored until 1948 and never ran as a full set again. The 16-seater Beavertails were given a second lease of life on the West Highland Line in 1956, but their sloping observation ends were found to offer only limited views, so BR rebuilt them at Cowlairs works in 1959 with more angled ends and added larger windows. Both Beavertails survived into preservation. No. 1729 was bought by the Gresley Society in 1966, and No. 1719 by John Cameron for his Lochty Private Railway two years later.

No. 1729 then spent several years running on the Keighley & Worth Valley Railway as No. 23 and in 1978 was bought by the late Sir William McAlpine, who took it to the former Steamtown museum at Carnforth, where it passed into the ownership of West Coast Railways founder David Smith. By then the observation end had rotted, and after a failed restoration attempt it was acquired by Great Central Railway-based Railway Vehicle Preservations in 2006. Asbestos was then removed from it by Knightsrail at Shoeburyness.

By then, Rothley-based Railway Vehicle Preservations had acquired sister Beavertail No. 1719E (its later BR number) and raised £60,000 through an appeal to restore it to its latter-day BR form in maroon livery. It entered GCR traffic on May 5, 2007. Railway Vehicle Preservations sold No. 1729 to Jeremy the year before. He funded the first stages of its restoration, before passing ownership to the Royal Scot Locomotive & General Trust.

The job of rebuilding No. 1729 was handed to Nemesis Rail in December 2007, the company then based at Barrow Hill, but subsequently moving to Burton-on-Trent.

By far the largest challenge was the rebuilding of the sloping end of the coach, completely from scratch. Nemesis embarked on one of the most thorough and complex projects to rebuild a heritage railway vehicle ever attempted. Once completed, No. 1729 was moved inside the One:One Collection museum and placed for short-term safe storage until COVID-19 pandemic restrictions were eased, alongside *Bittern*, while being offered for hire to heritage lines. It has been fitted only with vacuum braking, and while it would be technically possible to get permission for it to run on the main line, there are no plans to do so because of the expense and complexity of getting permission for a wooden-bodied vehicle to be registered accordingly. Yet would it not look magnificent, coupled to a rake of LNER teak coaches, such as those at the North Yorkshire moors Railway, for instance?

One hundred extra car parking spaces were added at Grantham station in 2021 as part of a £1.50m scheme of improvements. The new car park was laid on formerly disused land just a short walk from the centre of town — and given a name — Mallard.

Gresley's A4s became legends in their own lifetime and are destined to be fabled icons in perpetuity. As the 100th anniversary of the steam railway speed record run, which is unlikely ever to be beaten, appears on the distant horizon in 2038, the question will inevitable be asked — might *Mallard* be resteamed for it? And will all six A4s ever meet again? Never say never — because you then run the risk of another Steve Davies deciding otherwise! He proved that yet again, railway preservation has shown itself to be the art of the possible, and in so doing he created one of the most successful events in the history of the National Railway Museum, reinforcing its own standing as a world market leader.

Index